fr Eleni

Blessings + love from

Grma

My Father,
Maker of the Trees

My Father,
Maker of the Trees

How I Survived the Rwandan Genocide

Eric Irivuzumugabe

with Tracey D. Lawrence

BakerBooks
a division of Baker Publishing Group
Grand Rapids, Michigan

In Loving Memory

This book is dedicated to all my family members who lost their lives during the 1994 genocide, though the list is greater than the seventy names here.

Then Peter came to Jesus and asked, "Lord, how many times shall I forgive my brother when he sins against me? Up to seven times?" Jesus answered, "I tell you, not seven times, but seventy-seven times."

Matthew 18:21–22

Honoring you in Jesus Christ,
Eric

1. Senyamakweshi Nazri
2. Nyirasoni Félicitée
3. Mutegwamaso Drocelle
4. Muvubyi Emmanuel
5. Nyiramajigija Verediane
6. Kanakuze Mediatrice
7. Umutesi Shushu
8. Muhongayire
9. Murindwa
10. Dusabumuremyi Cyriaque
11. Mwenzikazi Vestine
12. Mukandirima Drocelle
13. Mujawamariya
14. Mujawayezu
15. Rebero
16. Munganyinka
17. Nyirakobwa
18. Sehaya Népomucènne
19. Mukarugema Caritas
20. Christine
21. Rujayana
22. Mukanyonga Boudensianne
23. Ryogori Xavier
24. Rurangangabo Jean Paul
25. Kizayire Helena
26. Shyaka
27. Seromba Noël
28. Nkusi Emmanuel
29. Munyaneza
30. Musengimana
31. Mukunzi
32. Gikudiro Senkunda
33. Rwiyamirira Augustin
34. Musanabera Verena
35. Gikudiro Rwiyamirira
36. Dukunde
37. Ruhumuriza
38. Sekidende
39. Ruhigura
40. Ntagungira
41. Rutuku
42. Remera
43. Higiro
44. Kamanzi Charles
45. Venantie
46. Mukankusi
47. Gakecuru
48. Agnès
49. Bushayija Théoneste
50. Munyeshuri Samuel
51. Nyirakanyana Espérance
52. Frère Jean Baptiste
53. Mukamurenzi Patricien
54. Mukamuganga Marie Jeanne
55. Dusabimana Claudine
56. Ruzindana Leonard
57. Kayitare Augustin
58. Kayitare Daniel
59. Kamandwa Jean
60. Rurangirwa Ephrem
61. Oliva Jolie
62. Vuguziga Mado
63. Shumbusho Figil
64. Iyakaremye
65. Kanyonga Concesca
66. Uwibambe
67. Rafiki
68. Muhashyi Daniel
69. Gacakiranyi Caravel
70. Mudaheranwa Joseph

© 2009 by Eric Irivuzumugabe

Published by Baker Books
a division of Baker Publishing Group
P.O. Box 6287, Grand Rapids, MI 49516-6287
www.bakerbooks.com

Printed in the United States of America

Library of Congress Cataloging-in-Publication Data
Irivuzumugabe, Eric.
    My father, maker of the trees : how I survived the Rwandan genocide / Eric Irivuzumugabe ; with Tracey D. Lawrence.
        p.   cm.
    ISBN 978-0-8010-1320-1 (cloth)
    1. Irivuzumugabe, Eric. 2. Christian biography—Rwanda. 3. Genocide—Rwanda. 4. Rwanda—History—Civil War, 1994. I. Lawrence, Tracey D. II. Title.
    BR1720.I75A3   2009
    276.7571'0829092—dc22   2009013820
    [B]

Contents

7

Acknowledgments

I wish to thank my family members who survived the period of genocide in 1994, including my brothers Mugabo Egide and Murinzi Daniel. They have always been close to me and given their moral support. They encouraged me when I was discouraged in the course of searching for the relevant stories to put in the book, and they even gave me their love. The other members still in my family are my uncles Rudakubana Innocent, Nyombayire Jean Marie Vianney, and Ruyombyana Canisius, and my aunts are Mukamana Esperance and Mukandori Cecile.

I thank also my dear pastors in Restoration Church, including Pastor Ndagijimana Joshua Masasu, Pastor Mukwiza Siméon, Pastor Jean Bosco Habimana, Pastor Ruhimbya Aaron, and Pastor Ntizimira Déo, who all together played an important role in shaping my life, each one being like a father to me. They helped me both spiritually and physically by accepting me as a son, and this acceptance built my hope in God, which resulted in my trusting in the Word of God as revealed to me, so I could become a blessing to many people, especially orphans.

I thank my family in Wisconsin, Joie and Douglas and their whole family, who always showed me love and care as my parents, brothers, and sisters. I also thank Gerri and Greg Kier for the help they offered while I was in Colorado during the process of writing this book.

I would like to thank other people who worked hard to make this book a success: sister Tracey, for doing a lot of writing; Mark, for working as an agent; and Baker Publishing Group for publishing this book. I appreciate the great work and commitment and all the necessary contributions these people made for this book project. We could not have communicated without our interpreters: Aime Ndayitabi, Gakuba Fiston, and Gasana Parfait.

Last but not least, I would like to thank Humura Ministries leaders and members Murekatete Vestine, Nkurunziza Godfrey, Tushabe Jane, Ngabonziza Maurice, and others for the work they contributed in the process of producing this book, which is a big achievement for the ministry.

Eric Irivuzumugabe

I owe a great debt of gratitude to my supportive and loving husband, Noel, who serves our marriage with teamwork. I could not possibly have completed this project without his encouragement and support. I also wish to thank my beautiful son, Jack Brennan, who graced our lives three years ago.

His easygoing disposition makes it all the more possible to keep persevering through each book project.

I also wish to acknowledge my parents, Adolph and Sybil Diaz. Their prayer support and care for Jack during this project made it achievable for me to meet my deadline. And even more than that, their faith continues to inspire me and helps me to keep pressing on toward the real prize. Throughout my whole life, they've been the best of cheerleaders.

I'm grateful to my brother, Kevin, who accompanied me to Rwanda and served the vision of this book as well. He always gives me his thoughtful critique, and God has gifted him deeply with so many creative abilities that I continue to discover—he is a true Renaissance man.

To my amazement, God always faithfully provides for me a close friend who shares a special affinity with what I'm working on. Joy Schwarting, a dear friend in Christ, showed me support in every way possible for this book, though she juggles work and church activities and lovingly serves her husband, Steve, and their two precious boys, Sam and Jakey. She was there for me especially during crunch time.

I'm amazed at the way God introduced me to Joie and Douglas Pirkey, and I have been blessed to witness the depth of their commitment to the Rwandan people. This book would not have been possible without their faith and crazy love for God.

Finally I want to thank the stellar team at Baker Books, more specifically Chad Allen for his vision for Eric's story and his perseverance with me in shaping the manuscript. I'm also grateful for my agent, Mark Sweeney, and his wife, Janet, as they have supported me with great professionalism through the project. Without the support team I have mentioned, I doubt I would even have a page written.

And I'm grateful for Eric, as he had to trust at so many levels with so many cultural puzzles to figure out along the way. Eric, God will use your courage to trust in mighty ways.

Tracey D. Lawrence

Introduction

I feel in myself the future life. I am like a forest which has
been more than once cut down. The new shoots are livelier
than ever. I am rising toward the sky. The sunshine is on my
head. The earth gives me its generous sap, but heaven lights
me with its unknown worlds.

Victor Hugo

In my country, the cypress tree is known as "the tree of life."
As a child I admired these trees, which gave a beautiful bor-
der to my village. Like most boys, I found shade and pleasure in their beauty, often sitting at a bulky trunk with my
thoughts and dreams. I also could never resist a good climb
into their branches, imagining I was a mighty soldier escaping the enemy. And when I was tired of being a soldier, I let
the staunch branches cradle me like a baby while I turned my
face toward the nurturing sun. After school, I longed to hike

to the steaming, rolling hills where the cypress trees stood in clusters. Brilliant sky covered my homeland, and my boyhood playground was paradise.

I never imagined that this place of childhood delight would become a battlefield. Never did I think a cypress tree would become the tree of survival for me. Never did I think its branches would save me from the bullets and machetes of hostile militia. I am still haunted by my past as the evils of genocide visit me in night terrors. For fifteen days and nights, I hid in terror from the outbreak of violence and raging devils who overtook my village. But I must tell you, this horror is only a portion of my story.

My name is Eric Irivuzumugabe, and I am a genocide survivor. My hope is that my story will bring you closer to the almighty God, who saved me from the trenches of evil. I am one of many Tutsi (pronounced *toot-see*) people who did not perish in the largest massacre of Rwanda. The heinous bloodthirst that invaded my homeland in April of 1994 is something I will always carry with me this side of heaven. But now God is also helping me to carry hope in my heart.

The evil of genocide is not something that can be easily explained. I still don't have a satisfying answer as to why humanity does not learn from history. Six million Jews were murdered at the hands of the Nazi regime just over sixty years ago. Over one million Tutsi people were murdered just over fifteen years ago. Holocausts continue to happen today, even in the modern world. Racism, hatred, and greed are alive in this fallen world as humanity continues to give itself over to empty and destructive ambitions. Because of hate, millions who bore the image of God have been slaughtered. Such evil is hard for most of us to grasp. Yet I know this: I serve a God who is not wasteful, and he is using my history to bring hope to others. Isaiah 55 reminds me that his ways are higher than mine, and so the mystery of suffering will continue to be with me until his return. I know he saved me from the hands of my enemy so that I might serve my hurting generation. I know now that his sovereign signature marks every tree. I believe God spared my life to extend hope beyond the borders of Rwanda, to orphans, to those who have lost family, to those who feel like God has abandoned them.

No matter what your current circumstances may be or what trials you face today, I am living proof that God can take a shattered life and breathe new life into a broken heart. My hope for you is that as you read my story, you experience healing from past hurts in your own life and find God as your source of comfort. No one has to live as a victim. Whether you have to face the scars of abuse, have lost loved ones, or have physical or emotional pain every day, God sees you and has not forgotten you. He is waiting for you to reach out to him and answer the call that is on your life. I humbly offer my story to you so that you too might be convinced that the power of God is at work, even in the darkest of worlds.

PART 1
The Coming Threat

A Family of Survivors

The LORD will scatter you among the peoples, and only a
few of you will survive among the nations to which the LORD
will drive you.

Deuteronomy 4:27

I remember the day my grandfather gathered my whole family together to instruct us how to flee. "Be careful. Don't separate from each other. I know we will be killed, but stay together as a family at all costs. You will not be spared, but flee as best you can." He knew firsthand about the evil days we would have to face as Tutsi people.

I come from a family of survivors. The genocide of April 1994 was not the first in my country. My grandfather, Senyamakweshi Nazri, survived the genocides of 1959 and 1972. Considering the grim odds of survival, he shouldn't have lived to tell his personal accounts of those two massacres. Yet

19

Grandfather was alive to witness the evil cadence of genocide drawing near once again.

The terrors began on April 7, the day after our president's plane was gunned down. We were told to stay in the house; no one could go out and play. This was not an easy thing for my ten-year-old brother, Mugabo. I remember coming inside from the pasture with Mugabo and my uncle Canisius to find my other siblings already gathered. Umutesi Shushu, my fourteen-year-old sister, had been helping my mother tend to baby Murindwa, who had been crying. Murinzi Daniel, age six, had been peacefully napping on the floor. My sister Muhongayire, age eight, stopped her play with dolls to listen to what Grandfather was about to tell us.

We were all shocked to hear that our president, Juvénal Habyarimana , had died in a plane crash. We weren't sure who was behind the assassination, whether it was Tutsi rebels or Hutu extremists. Regardless, it set into motion the bloodiest one hundred days our country has ever known.

Warnings of the coming threat surrounded Mburabuturo, our village. You could feel the tension as family members scurried to one another, whispering plans of escape. We knew genocide was coming again to Rwanda. The Hutu extremists, known as the Interahamwe, had begun their manhunt. It would be only a short time before they would reach the region of Rwamagana where all my relatives lived.

A cloud of smoke drifted down to the valley, and we could see houses burning in surrounding villages. I could taste the soot and ash, carried by the brewing storm; we knew it was time to leave our homes. I could see our dear neighbor Kimonyo Antoine's home on the outskirts of town disappear into the raging flames. The enemy quickly began looting, killing, and destroying homes, beginning at the edge of the hills and working their way through the village to dominate every Tutsi home until all was destroyed. The evil drone of violence grew closer and closer by the moment. My mother, my brothers and sisters, my aunts and uncles, and my cousins all headed together down a path that Grandfather showed us. We took nothing with us except our beloved dairy cow, Indibori ("multicolored"), in hopes of providing milk for any surviving children. That was the last time we all would be together.

My Boyhood

As a boy, I was very happy. The rivers laughed with me as I followed their courses at play. Rwanda's orangey-red soil nourished my family's crops of maize, coffee, and banana trees. We were very blessed. I always had plenty to eat and plenty of love. We were a close family, and I was especially close to my father, Nkubana John. He was a businessman and farmer who lived generously—he gave when his harvest was bountiful and when it was sparse. In fact, when he really liked someone in our village, he would give them a cow. He sold coffee, bananas, and other crops to help support our family. Everyone liked Nkubana John, who was known for his agreeable disposition and fun-loving sense of humor.

I could tell my father anything; he knew I was a serious boy. I wanted to be seen as responsible, and I wanted to grow up to be like him, a man respected and admired.

In Rwanda, our roads are not just a place for transportation and automobiles; they are where we walk as friends and family, sharing our thoughts and building relationships. My father and I enjoyed daily outings on those roads, walking up and down the hilly countryside. He often knew what I was going to say before I spoke.

I was a contemplative young boy, so I asked a lot of questions about life, where it was going to lead me, and what my purpose might be. He knew what bothered me and was very attentive to my feelings. Our routine walks helped me unravel my ponderings, and they provided a rhythm in my day that settled me.

When I began to ask questions about the prejudices I experienced in school, my father began to share the history of genocide in Rwanda with me. Tension between Hutus and Tutsis wasn't anything new to my homeland. As rumors of another genocide plot began to increase, we talked more and more about this evil. I began to understand why schools were segregated and why I didn't feel like I had the same rights as some of my Hutu classmates. My father explained carefully to me that we were Tutsis, and that many Hutus wanted to kill us and dominate our country. He shared with me stories about relatives I had not met who were forced to flee to safety in other African countries.

"Father, my relatives who are living as refugees, are they okay? . . . Do you think such persecution could still happen to us today?"

"Yes, Eric. I must be honest. Genocide could happen again."

"Is this persecution you are telling me about the reason you didn't go to university? Will I not be able to go to university?"

"My dear son, I know your heart is to continue your education. You are so bright, and I know you would excel in college, but I must tell you the truth. You are not likely to go because you are Tutsi. We are not given the same opportunities as Hutus."

Though I could not fully understand such hatred as a nine-year-old boy, I felt secure knowing my father loved me and would take care of us. On my walks home from school, I found my thoughts wandering back to things my father said, and I tried to figure out what genocide really was. My thoughts began to gather as a dark cloud that overshadowed my boyhood. As my father continued to tell me of the persecution he had experienced as a boy and as a man, my own awareness of the evil of prejudice rapidly increased.

School became very difficult for me. All the students were given identification cards that classified us as Hutu or Tutsi. They wanted us to be divided, but as innocent children we befriended one another. I remember the way teachers would punish Tutsi children. Often we were removed from the classroom, though we had done nothing wrong. The teacher would make us go outside so we could not learn like the Hutu children. To me this was the cruelest form of punishment and hard to accept as a young boy eager to learn. No matter how well I performed, I never achieved enough in the eyes of my Hutu teachers. My school was once a place where I felt freedom to discover and dream, but right before the genocide, it became a place that smothered my ambitions. With my father's help and encouragement, I desperately tried to rise above the discrimination I felt.

Young Dreams

Before the genocide, my father knew I was suffering from the same painful treatment he had experienced throughout his life, but he always tried to remain positive, to believe and hope for a bright future. Around the time the persecution started, he asked me what I wanted to be when I grew up. Since college was not possible, I said I wanted to be a driver and chauffeur people around. Most people in Rwanda do not have cars. As a boy, along with my brothers and sisters, I used to play with colored wire that could be bent into different animals and objects. Mine always ended up being a car of some kind.

Despite the discrimination around me, I was a content child. I had many friends and was well liked in my village. The younger generations didn't feel the tribal tensions—we all just wanted to play together. Relationally I was very rich. My family gave me the nickname Kidamage, which means "beautiful child." Sometimes it was embarrassing when my mother called out, "Kidamage!" in front of my soccer friends.

Soccer was one of my favorite pastimes, and I loved to be out on the hills with my soccer ball whenever I could. If I wasn't chasing a ball, I was just roaming outside. Whether I was with my friends, chasing a storm, or alone chasing my private dreams, the bush was where I felt most alive. My favorite subjects in school were science and history. I enjoyed trying to figure out the world, exploring what might be possible.

I'm grateful for my memories of family, especially those I have of my father. He did not have to endure the genocide of 1994, as he became ill and died before the militia began to attack. I had always cherished any time I could be with him—talking, playing, or reading. He helped me plant dreams in my heart. He used to read me the Bible. Because he liked it, I began to enjoy reading it on my own too.

I was very young, so I don't recall the exact details or even what kind of illness my father had, but I remember going to the hospital in Kigali where he died. I remember the last thing he said to me: "Eric, be strong and courageous. You can be a hero to many." Losing him broke my heart. We buried him back in our village. His last loving words have stayed alive in my heart, even through the sinister days of genocide. I hear my father's voice echo in me even now.

Though I had lost my father and grieved like so many in our village, I never felt like an orphan. We were able to survive because we had a strong family that surrounded us with support. Everyone helped my mother provide for me and my brothers and sisters so that she would not have to work. My grandparents and aunts and uncles all shared their income, while my mother continued to care for all six of us. Life was good in my village, despite the growing threat of genocide. We continued to laugh, cry, celebrate, and carry on as a family. My sister wrote beautiful poetry; my mother sang like an angel and danced gracefully. Sometimes we all danced for hours, trying to muster up the grace our mother possessed. No one could dance like she danced.

Rumors of attack tried to rob us of our future hopes; instinctively we fought to hold on to the splendor that surrounded us, the everyday beauty that we were meant to stop and notice.

Tribal Tensions

The strife between the Hutu and Tutsi people has been a bitter seed plaguing my country for decades. In the 1920s Belgian ethnologists analyzed the skulls of Tutsis and Hutus and declared the Tutsi people to be the superior tribe. They redefined who we were, telling Rwandans how each tribe should view themselves, and they were threatened by the fact that we were a unified country, cohabiting as peace-loving neighbors. From the 1920s through the 1960s, the Germans and Belgians ruled Rwanda indirectly through Tutsi monarchs and chiefs. Prejudices and fabrications continued for decades, severing relationships, as some adopted the colonialists' belief that the superior "race" were Tutsi because they were from northeast Africa—Egypt or Abyssinia (Ethiopia).

By the 1930s the colonizers conducted a census, and Rwandans adopted an identity card system indicating ethnicity—Tutsi, Hutu, or Twa (pigmy). These identities were ingrained in our Rwandese culture up to 1994. In the 1958 "Hutu Manifesto," Hutu leaders declared that the tribes were different races, which demonstrates how embedded the ideology had become, for in reality we were the same race. Tutsis and Hutus spoke the same language, shared in the same religions, and intermarried. These unfounded prejudices paralyzed our country with sinful sentiments of dominance, subordination, exploitation, and suffering.

The truth is, it is difficult to tell who is Tutsi and who is Hutu by outward characteristics. According to Belgian colonists, typically Tutsi were thought to be tall, fairer-skinned, and more elegant in stature. Hutus were generalized as short, flat-nosed, darker-skinned people. The Belgians imposed their authority over the Hutus and elevated the Tutsi people, causing Rwandans to become a divided people. The colonists knew a divided country could not stand, and indeed the country began to be destroyed by this evil ideology. Genocide broke out in 1959 and in 1972 as hostile feelings continued to rise among the tribes. No battle the Interahamwe (Hutu extremists) executed was just. There was only one aggressor. Tutsis fought only to survive. Ultimately, no one would declare victory, for genocide has no victors.

The colonists' dogma never left the minds of Rwandans, generation after generation. Such dynamics caused genocide to reoccur in 1994. This genocide was carried out primarily by two extremist Hutu militia groups, the Interahamwe ("those who fight together") and the Impuzamugambi ("those with the same goal") during about one hundred days, from April 7 through mid-July 1994.

Over one million people died.

The Outbreak

For most genocide survivors, it is not easy to remember the days of the outbreak. Some of my family members are still too traumatized to share their account of survival. The pain is still raw. Flashbacks haunt the nights. Migraines are common for many who try to recall the bloody details. My family's story is mentally challenging for me to share even now. As I prepare to speak of the hardest days of survival, tears wet my face. I know I need God's strength to help me tell of my horrors. I tell my story, ultimately, to bring healing to my heart and to every heart that has been wounded. I want to give my pain to God as an offering so that I can comfort others, but it is hard.

The sounds of violence roared through the countryside. Our days of playful frolic and daydreaming were interrupted. Evil surrounded us, and Grandfather knew most of his family would not survive. Forty of us made our way up an unknown path my grandfather showed us; it led us to the nearby hills where we hoped to find a hiding place.

That's when we heard their shrill voices. "Don't let anyone escape! Capture *all* the cockroaches!" shouted the Interahamwe. Hill by hill, the killers wiped out all that was good and beautiful.

Before I left my village, I was able to prepare for what I might have to endure. I went inside my home for the last time, layering on my body five shirts and several pairs of pants for warmth at night and protection from the elements. It was all I could stand, and I knew any more clothing would slow me down.

We tried to stay paired up with someone in our family; our chances of survival diminished greatly if we separated. All the stories of genocide I had heard from my father and grandfather flooded my mind as I fled, gasping for air. Why was this happening again? We knew our homes were the most unsafe place to be now, but I desperately wanted to turn back for shelter under my own roof. I never saw my home again.

In about an hour we reached the mountainside, which was just beyond the hills my family owned. The violence overtook our village more rapidly than expected: some Tutsis were already wounded, some were comatose from shock, and some who had been shot died on the climb up. There was no time to bury our loved ones, so against the fiber of our souls, we buried our emotions instead as we ran from death. Terror was blowing through the thick foliage, and the fear I felt with each breath was paralyzing. All around us we heard the rage of violence, the looting, the cries for help. The smoke grew thicker as homes continued to go up in flames.

We knew the Interahamwe was beginning to overtake the bush. The cows that families had taken with them were being slaughtered. I frantically tried to remember where I had last seen my brother Mugabo Egide. He loved our cows, especially Indibori. Egide used to run all the way home from school, planting himself along the road to watch the cows. He could imitate Indibori's slow sway as she munched on the green fields like she owned my father's land. Once he told me she had twenty-nine patches of brown on one side and seven white patches on her stomach. Egide talked with the cows, milked them, and sometimes tried to ride them. He loved everything about them. I hoped that Indibori and Egide were safe somewhere.

As we heard the cries of the terrorized animals, we knew our killers were drawing close. Young calves were searching for their mothers, trumpeting out in fear. Herds were searching for their families just as all of us were. Panic spread across the hills.

Flashbacks on the Run

My grandfather had told me many times before of how he and some of my family survived previous genocides. I had heard of the brutality of 1959 and 1972, how the radical Hutus were resolved to eradicate every Tutsi. And now the demons of the past were once again here, terrorizing my family. I was now walking in the ghostlike, tormenting steps of my ancestors.

My grandfather once told me about the 1959 genocide. My aunt had been born just before the killing started—baby Musanabera Verena. The extremist Hutus took her out of the sling on her mother's back. They scalped her infant head, harassed her, and left them both for dead. They showed no mercy toward any Tutsi, not even babies. Somehow, Aunt Verena and her mother survived. Grandfather was able to escape too, taking baby Verena and my father to the Congo where they would be safe. Some days they hid in different churches, and other days just wherever they could find refuge, away from the killings. I remembered this story as I ran, and I clung to the resilience of my ancestors. I hoped for survival, though I knew it was not likely.

On the first day of our flight, the militia had not yet fully surrounded the mountain where we were. We had a little time to plan how we might stay alive. It was not safe for women to be with the men or young boys of the family, because the militia was more aggressively slaughtering males. So Grandfather helped the men prepare for how we would care for the women of the family and determine who should flee together. Recalling how he had escaped previous genocides, Grandfather believed that if we remained hidden, we might live. The idea was to move away from the village and remain out of sight until the violence passed. But that meant staying on the move. And so all day and night we kept changing our location.

Fueled by Fear

On the evening of the second day, our fears were realized. The militia made their way into the hills with their brutish guns and weapons, hunting for Tutsi blood. About thirty hunters were killing close to our hiding place. Gunshot blasts rang through the bush, sending waves of shock through my heart and stomach. I had never heard a gun so close to me before. Because my family made for a small crowd and could be spotted easily on the hill, we knew we were a target for their hateful ridicule and would be found. We knew we needed to reach the masses of Tutsis farther up the hills before we would feel safer.

Huddling together in the bush, we tried to form our own stronghold against the enemy—the unshakable love we had for each other. Though we knew we had to stay silent, cries of terror were screaming through our veins. With clenched hands I held on to my beautiful family, terrified to let go.

About 150 of us, mostly my relatives, fled from our village. We learned quickly that the Interahamwe was not just looting and destroying Tutsi homes like in previous attacks—rumors were circulating that this time they were out to exterminate Tutsis.

We saw masses of people fleeing from one hill to the next. Thousands of us were gathering in hopes of finding refuge in numbers. Overwhelming numbers of Tutsi, maybe some twenty thousand, were struggling to make it to the next hill, Nyarusange. None of us had food or drink or any sophisticated strategies of survival. Running from the enemy was our strongest weapon.

Grandfather encouraged us to keep our focus on the next hill. He said, "If we get close to others, we will have more strength to fight." As we moved toward other fleeing Tutsis, we could hear others shouting out in terror. The noise was nauseating, chaotic, and numbing.

I remember my uncle, Ruyombyana Canisius, screaming out, "Why has my life been reduced to this? Why doesn't God do something about the killers?" He was eighteen years old at the time, just two years older than me.

We prepared ourselves to flee from our hiding place and separate. We knew we had to scatter at this point in order to survive. My grandmother gathered all the grandchildren, aunts, uncles, and siblings one last time. Grandmother was a strong woman, so she took charge of the young children of our family who could not run without help. Though she fearlessly protected her grandchildren, they were killed within days.

All at once we began running beyond our own strength, fueled by fear. I found myself almost instantly separated from everyone, but I managed to spot my grandfather. We fled and hid together. Grandfather knew the bush well and had outwitted the militia many times before. His keen sense of survival kept us safe during those hours, although I was so afraid my gasps for air and my pounding heart would give us away. Sharp pains shot up and down my calves, and my head was spinning as I tried to ignore the trail of dead villagers that I saw. My whole body felt burdened because I knew that many of my family members did not survive the second day of genocide.

Grandfather and I managed to find a place to hide together until morning. Like rabid wolves, the militia raided the area, and we were uncertain at this point where my grandmother and many of the others had gone. We had lost touch with everyone. Grandfather lamented being separated from his wife and his children, so that night we decided to go back to where we thought they might be.

The killers had left the bush for the night, and we no longer felt the burning blasts of hell shooting out from every direction. We soon heard timid, rustling noises and found a cluster of Tutsi people in hiding. Peering into the black atmosphere, it was hard to see if our family was there. Finally we found Grandmother and some others. We all quietly exchanged our encounters of escape and learned that other men from our family were still alive. Because men were still the main target, we knew that the women and children would not be safe if we stayed there too long. So Grandfather and I left around 3:00 a.m. to go back to our hiding place.

Early in the afternoon we heard shots, then hostile voices, coming from the area where we had left our family. Grandfather and I knew that our family was being attacked; the anguish we felt because we couldn't protect them was depleting our energy. We spent that day and another night hiding before it was safe to go back to see if our family had survived. Grandfather's strength was waning, and I knew no words could comfort him. He had been face-to-face with this same hatred generations before. I wondered how his heart could bear seeing such butchery again. Some of my uncles went back to investigate. Several of my relatives were seriously wounded, struggling to survive.

The militia was now overtaking the mountainside once again. We heard the Hutus coming for us, and we had to scatter, skirt away from them, and hide in the small bushes around the hills. Here I huddled with my grandfather and my cousin Munyaneza, thankful to have survived another day but quietly grieving for all those we lost. Fatigue and emotional stress were beginning to take their toll on all of us. We spent another night and day there trying to rest, though our minds could never shut out the violence that encircled us. Somehow we had survived about five days of fleeing. We woke again only to hear the Hutu extremists searching for more Tutsi blood.

Some of my family members became physically ill, even before we left the village, as they anticipated their death. But after a few days passed, we had felt fear so long that we no longer recognized it as fear. Horrific sounds kept coming at us: children crying out for food, children crying because they saw their mothers murdered, and mothers shrieking in anguish as their sons died in their arms. Every day the sounds of hate came hurling at us. Day and night, the screams continued and led us all toward madness.

Hillside Massacre

Even the women in the Interahamwe were instructed to kill the Tutsi children. They would spy on the hills and tell the militia where there were more families in hiding. We could hear the Hutu women shouting across the mountains to the killers, "Go over there. You will find more to kill."

Thousands of Tutsis were on the hill, now over twenty thousand of us. Grenades were thrown into the masses from multiple directions at once, while other militia groups were shooting rounds and rounds of ammunition. Everyone was forced to run, though there was no clear path to safety. Smoke burned in our lungs, and the fires were blinding.

It felt torturous to keep running, but it was all I could do. Twenty people, five people, fifteen people at a time were all falling down in front of me, tripping me, but I just kept running. Women were falling behind because they couldn't keep ahead of their hunters. Tutsi people were plunging to the ground everywhere. Neighbors, cousins, aunts, just falling, some exhausted, some dead.

I saw my uncle Canisius running every which way. As I kept tripping over corpses, I caught sight of Canisius's head wound and his bloody shoulder as he fell and grabbed his leg. I wanted to scream out his name, but I just kept running in circles. Many times a familiar face from my village would flash in front of me in the midst of the mayhem, and then in seconds it was gone. At this time we all had to run alone if we were going to survive. But at night our instinct was to cluster so we could comfort one another. I always searched for my grandfather during these times.

This was one of the bloodiest days in Rwandan history. This particular massacre was one of the largest, and I have blocked out most of it from my memory. As I strain to remember what happened on the hillside, a day that seemed to be the devil's win, there's one haunting memory that I cannot suppress. When my grandfather heard one of his sons being taken captive, he gave up his desire to live; he resigned to become their prey. Enduring three genocides in his lifetime was beyond what anyone would consider humanly possible. We heard from others hiding nearby how my uncle was killed.

My grandfather could not bear the loss of his son. Later that night, Grandfather went alone to check on Grandmother and our family.

"Stay here. You must not come with me. Even if I'm killed, it is better for you to be spared. You have your whole lives to live," reasoned Grandfather.

My cousins and I obeyed reluctantly, but that was the last time we saw him.

Later we overheard other Tutsis hiding in the bush talking about the confrontation that had taken place. My grandfather fell into the hands of the corrupted officers of the government, who turned him over to the militia to be killed. In his delirious state, he began to speak boldly to the Hutu extremists. They harassed my grandfather, interrogating him.

"Where are you coming from, old man?" said one Hutu soldier.

"Where are you headed?" others maliciously asked.

"You killers are evil beasts, but I will not die in fear of you!" said my grandfather in defiance. "You rob us for no reason, and yet your appetite to harm never ceases. How can you kill a God-fearing man like my son who has done you no harm? Come get me. You cannot take my manhood away. Why can't you learn from the mistakes of your evil ancestors? You are not human!"

Grandfather held back nothing; all the years of rage and emotion from previous genocides came out.

They savagely murdered my grandfather with machetes and swords, dismembering his limbs. The militia was never satisfied to just shoot someone when there was an opportunity to torture a Tutsi. They gloated in the pain and celebrated over the spilled blood like demon-possessed savages.

My cousin and I waited until about 2:00 p.m. that next day, but soon we heard the militia coming frightfully close to our hiding place. We separated and began to run as fast as we could, but Munyaneza could not outrun them. I knew if I looked back, I would fall. I had to just keep running. . . .

Alone in the Bush

I never saw my cousin again. We were both sixteen years old, still boys. Munyaneza and I had grown up together, sharing many boyhood pleasures. After a few games of soccer, we'd pick mangoes and see who could eat the most. He always won. I couldn't imagine life without him.

Though I was struggling to bear the profound grief in my heart, I fiercely ran to the jungle and stayed there through the night, terrorized, disoriented, and alone. Pushed up against a tree, I felt my colored-wire car poke through my back pocket—the one reminder I snatched from our home to celebrate my boyhood. I caressed the toy and held it close to my chest, letting my mind wander back to a happy time, trying to rest.

I remembered how Canisius and I would perch ourselves against the fence that corralled our family's livestock and watch people go by while we manipulated the wires into new treasures. We could laugh for hours at our creations, trying to outdo one another in originality. One time Canisius tried to form the shape of Mugabo Egide, me, and himself from one piece of wire. For the wire to accommodate us, he had to make each of us share an arm. I didn't tell him, but I thought it was beautiful and artistic.

Mugabo knew where to find us bigger boys and always wanted to be included. His eyes were electric with wonder as he held up a piece of wire and asked the same thing every day: "Eric, please make a cow for me." I would happily grant his request, but before I could finish the hind legs, he was already asking for another. I reached a point where I would make cows in my bed at night, just to have them for Mugabo the next day. To my amazement, he named each and every cow I made.

Clutching the wire toy, I tried to remember which direction Uncle Canisius ran the last time I saw him on the hillside, but I was uncertain if he had made it into the bush alive. The day's events circled my head in confusion. I had not seen Mugabo Egide during this God-forsaken string of days on the hillside. My family was quickly fading away from my life, receding entirely into boyhood memories.

In just a few days, most Tutsis from my village had been eradicated. I was unsure which of my family members had survived. I longed for my mother and wished I were safe in her comforting arms. I hoped that my two sisters and three brothers somehow were spared. I whispered their names through the night as I tried to rest my eyes. *Mugabo Egide . . . Murinzi Daniel . . . Murindwa . . . Umutesi Shushu . . . Muhongayire . . .* and my beloved mother, *Kanakuze Mediatrice.*

I read my Bible as a boy, but in this night of terror, I could find no trace of a loving or merciful God. Such a God seemed like a distant fairytale. The only thing that seemed real was the void in my heart and the cold jungle rain beating against my bruised skin. Thinking about God seemed like a foolish notion, and I didn't believe he cared about me. *How could a merciful God allow such devastation to happen to a country? How could he allow a beautiful family to perish in such a violent way?* Looking back, I now can see his hand guiding me through the dark of that night. Though I couldn't see him, he was present, lurking in the bush with me, chasing after my heart.

> I will give you the treasures of darkness,
>   riches stored in secret places,
> so that you may know that I am the LORD,
>   the God of Israel, who summons you by name.
>
> Isaiah 45:3

PART 2
A Thousand Escapes

Interlude

Three Streams Make a Mighty River

There is a river whose streams make glad the city of God,
the holy place where the Most High dwells.

Psalm 46:4

The following days and weeks of genocide were now about
surviving alone. Few clusters of families were hiding in the
bush together as most did not survive the hillside. Children
were running with strangers—most of us were running
alone.

With the help of God, I want to share three miraculous
stories of escape: the stories of three boys who survived despite facing every evil force imaginable. As I begin to recall
the narrow escapes we individually experienced, I realize there
is no rational answer to why we survived. The only way I can
try to understand is to appeal to the mystery of this life and
the sovereignty of God.

God laid out our courses of escape. Our stories are different and yet the same. They diverged and then by God's sovereignty came together as we struggled to keep running. Each of us ran toward our death what seemed to be a thousand times or more, yet we escaped again and again. Though we were separated, we were never far away from one another. Looking back, I marvel when I read Psalm 17: "My steps have held to your paths; my feet have not slipped" (v. 5). Only God knew where each of us could find the sure footing we needed to survive.

I was sixteen, Mugabo Egide was only ten, and my uncle Ruyombyana Canisius was eighteen. We were like three lonely streams running separately. We were unaware that our courses would dump into one mighty river. The winding turns of genocide would hold different terrors for each of us, but a Source bigger than ourselves kept us alive, running the race that was predestined for each of us to endure.

There is something powerful about hearing these three stories of escape as one testimony. I believe that together, our stories can uproot things in people's hearts that shouldn't be buried there. God continues to show me that the rush of the three separate courses pouring into one Source has the power to clean out impurities and open things up wider than just one stream alone could.

Entering the horrors of someone's personal escape from genocide is one of the most difficult things a heart can bear. But I've found that telling the testimonies of my brother and uncle has strengthened me to tell mine. Though fear and darkness have tried to consume my heart, an incandescent light hovers now over my family's story when I'm willing to share it with others. I know now that evil cannot destroy my heart, even as I remember its force again and again. As you read the accounts of terrorizing escape, don't let the darkness overtake you. I know this to be true: the River's grace sings louder and is much more powerful. The hellish killing ground could not thwart God's plan.

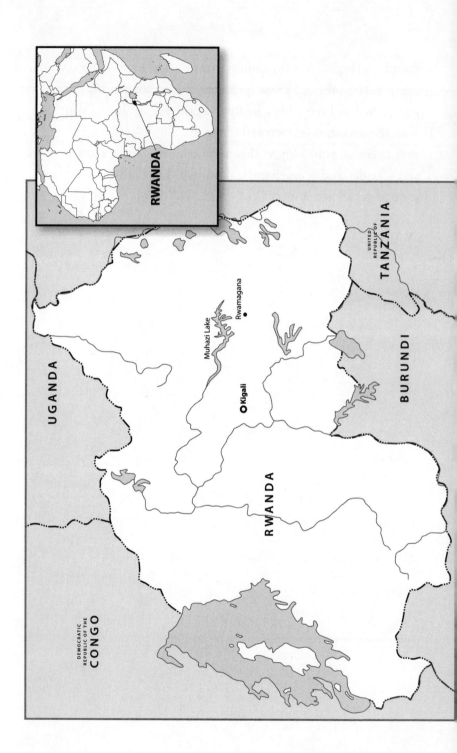

Eric

Life in the Trees

Every tree is sovereignly planted by God for a reason bigger
than we know.

Uncle Innocent

I fell asleep thinking the sun wouldn't rise again after the
hillside massacre. But when the intense light hit my face, I
knew it was time to run. I could feel the heavy weight of my
clothing from the previous night's downpour, so I took off
a couple layers to lighten my back and relieve my tired legs.
Quickly, I buried a shirt and a pair of pants so I would leave
no trail. I didn't know which direction to go. No place was
safe, and I was running out of options for shelter. I knew the
Interahamwe was going to come in hundreds over the hills,
and I had to stay hidden.

Intoxicated with hatred, the Interahamwe continued to
torture and kill Tutsis without respect for human life. No

form of death was too cruel, and the larger group massacres continued on. Tutsis were dragged from the backs of trucks. Thousands of young girls and women were raped and beaten to death. Rape was one of the fiercest weapons that the Interahamwe used as a strategy in destroying the Tutsi population. Most victims had to endure profound humiliation before they were killed. Some were buried alive in sewer holes.

As I ran, flashbacks of the previous months swarmed in my mind, particularly the rumors that had started in our village regarding an organized militia. I remembered the many times I would hear a bus full of Hutus go by, chanting their war songs against the Tutsi people:

> We are going to finish them
> We are going to clean them up
> We are going to finish all of them
> We are going to take them home
> This is not their home

Such mantras used to fill the bars at night in the coming and going of any ordinary day, years before the 1994 genocide began. Hutus, drunk on banana beer, exposed their hearts and sang of their intent to kill. But no one knew for sure what would happen. We knew the tension between tribes was still a reality, but no one wanted to face the possibility of yet another massacre. The militia, with its secret trainings and fighting strategies, was waiting for the right time to unleash its terror.

The Interahamwe was actively organizing with the help of the Hutu-led government. The young radical Hutus secretly trained in the day and quietly went home at night. Though they were not the most skilled or the best-trained fighters, their strength came from their united purpose, which was to decimate the Tutsi people.

As I kept running I remembered all that had felt strange before—the sudden chills I felt when walking by Hutus, the eerie threat of their chanting. It finally came together in my head that this was an elaborate plan of the devil himself.

I stopped to catch my breath and hoped that my head would stop pounding. I found a sturdy rock to sit on in the sun to rid myself of the stale rain left on my clothes. My eldest uncle, Uncle Innocent, was hiding in the nearby cluster of trees and spotted me out in the open, but it wasn't safe yet for him to make his presence known to me. He also knew that I was safe for this moment, as the militia was not nearby.

I'm not sure how long I sat on the rock. But it felt good to press against something solid that could hold up my weary body.

When darkness came, Uncle Innocent came down from the cypress tree to greet me. "Don't worry, Eric, it's me! Canisius and your other uncles are here too."

In my bewildered state, it was strange to hear a familiar voice call to me in the dark. I couldn't believe it was him! We didn't talk for fear of being heard, but with relief I followed my uncle to a safe area in the bush. Here I was reunited with all three surviving uncles. In the later hours of the night, we spoke to one another. We knew the militia was heading back to their homes, getting drunk and bragging of their day's kill.

"I'm amazed we are all here together after being scattered," Uncle Innocent said. "Maybe if the militia comes and finds us here, we at least will die together."

Being reunited, though we knew it was unlikely that all of us would survive, these thoughts were like food and water to us. We feasted on one another's company, exchanging our stories of escape. At first no one spoke of it, but we all were sure we would not escape this place alive. Though the warring violence stopped for the night, I could still hear the screams of suffering babies and children.

When dawn approached, Uncle Innocent instructed me on which tree to climb and how to remain hidden during the day.

"I'm not going to climb the tree alone. I want to be with you," I pleaded.

"It's important for you to hide in another tree," Innocent responded with great conviction. "Your isolation may be the very thing that saves you. I'm not going to climb into a tree until you get in your own tree. Eric, it will be better that they find us one by one."

Where the Trees Stand Still

The first day of fifteen days in the tree was a relief. I didn't have to think about how far my next run would be. And though we could not talk, to know my uncles were nearby gave me strength. My pulse slowed down and my heart didn't feel as if it would burst out of my chest from exhaustion anymore. Though we had no food or water, I was content to just rest. I wasn't going to run anymore.

But it was very difficult to not be on the move. I felt a sense of helplessness in just hiding. Soon time became an enemy and my worry and anxiety intensified. I wondered what evils my brothers and sisters were facing—if they had been spared. I questioned whether hiding in the trees was really safe at all. Since I had no other choice, I was able to let go of some of the unknowns and trust the advice of my uncle, who knew that most people who were unable to survive were found in the bush and in holes. The trees were our only chance.

It was torture for me to be still during the day. My mind never rested, as I was worried that they would creep up from behind me without me noticing. Running felt safer to me, and it provided mental escape the tree did not.

I found myself in this vicious cycle of believing I would be okay, then moments later being stricken with panic and anxiety. At times I would pull myself together and an unexplainable strength would cover my heart. But when thoughts returned of the reality of the genocide below me and all the cruel ways the militia members were murdering the people of my village, fear settled in. I speculated how my baby brother, Murindwa, might be murdered, though I had no idea where he was or if he was even alive. I thought of my sisters, their beauty, and how the Hutu militia might destroy the light in their eyes.

Though I was thankful for moments of quiet, the isolation brought me deplorable thoughts of the enemy below. I was relieved when nightfall came, knowing we'd gather around the trunks of the trees and I wouldn't have to see all the death surrounding the hills.

April is the rainy season in Rwanda, and the cold leaves and muddy ground stiffened my muscles at night. We couldn't really sleep, but it was an opportunity to change positions and rest our arms from clutching the branches. I found myself drifting off to sleep a few times, but I kept remembering the fright of the day's killings, and I would wake up trembling. All was void and black in my soul, like the starless sky.

I wondered if my brother Mugabo was alone or if he was with family.

Strong Branches

> Why am I fighting to live, if I'm just living to fight?
> Why am I trying to see, when there ain't nothing in
>   sight?
> Why am I dying to live, if I'm just living to die?
>
> Tupac Shakur

I had only been in the trees two days, and my determination turned to anger. The uneven bark cut my legs as I tried to climb. I pressed every muscle in my body against the awkward trunk of the tree until it anchored me to reach for the next branch. I felt like all of nature was against me. As I looked down I could see rotting bodies littering the roads, the same roads that used to carry laughter as children would make their way to school and mothers would walk to sell the morning milk.

Alone with my thoughts, I really began to question, *Why am I trying to live? Why are my uncles fighting to survive?*

We knew each day that thousands more were dying. I was agnonized by the thoughts going around and around in my head. *I doubt any of my brothers and sisters have survived. Each day only brings more death. I know I will never see my beloved neighbors and friends again. Maybe we are the only ones left from my village. If we do survive, what reason would there be to live? How would we even try to make sense of life again?*

Just as night and day became neutral in my mind—neither was any better than the other; hope didn't rise with the sun or grow in the dark—so did life and death.

The day moved along slowly and then slower still. Around midday I heard a voice outside of myself telling me that I was supposed to accept the branches holding me up as a sovereign friend. I became more grateful for their protection from the reach of the devils below.

Trying to clear my mind, I focused on the tree. I chipped away at the bark around a branch within reach and watched the balmy sap rescue the wound. I thought about how it knew what to do, hoping this might be proof there was a maker of trees. How did it know to release the sap? Who was telling it to? I noticed a patch of dead branches to my left, where the enemy could just look up and clearly see me, so I started to pull from the thick cluster of branches behind me, throwing the needles and twigs on top of one another as best as I could with one arm.

Tiny insects ran through the maze of the bark, darting back and forth with purpose. I tried to follow just one to see how long I could trace its steps. A spider began to spin a web from a small branch above me. The silken thread dropped in front of me, and I wondered how such a small thread could hold the spider up as it bounced around to three different corners. Out it swung in front of me, back and forth until I could see a pattern. The spider crawled on my hand and paused, as if it were looking up at its creative work. This tree was a fortress to both the spider and me.

I began to list the attributes of the tree in my mind: Strong. Alive. A refuge. A majestic tower. And I wondered about the tree maker. Was he these things too?

I counted each branch and limb until my eyes reached the top. I stopped when I couldn't count anymore, when I was left gazing toward the open patch of sky.

On the fifth day we did not see any militia nearby, but the hills still echoed back to us unrestrained violence. The Hutu radicals were ordering Tutsis to come out of hiding in the neighborhoods nearby.

Children cried out for mercy, "Heavenly Father, come down and save us!"

Such cries for family members intensified, then slowly waned as most Tutsis witnessed the murders of the last of their relatives. The Hutus gave no thought to how many orphans would be left to survive on their own.

Hearing the screams of terror made coping with hunger, thirst, and fatigue all the more difficult. We had to keep telling ourselves to hold on tight to the branches. One day seemed like a year. I was convinced the sun was standing still to prolong the torture. Though I had been rather indifferent to God through this struggle, I did pray, as my grandfather had instructed us to do throughout our escape. Like the desperate prayers of the innocent children we heard, I too asked God to protect me and to fulfill his plan in my life.

Night finally came, but I almost didn't notice the full moon right in front of me. The same voice I had heard earlier reminded me to be thankful for this place of rest. After surviving so many battles below and so many battles of my will, I started to believe we were all led here by something greater than ourselves. Before I closed my eyes, I found the energy to chat with my uncles. The things I had once longed for in life were a blur. Simple conversation and hearing the voices of my loving uncles—this was all I needed.

We shared the hard moments we'd had in the day. "I felt like sleeping today," one of us would confess, and another would say, "I almost didn't come down tonight." We tried to shoulder our burdens together, and somehow we received enough encouragement to make the next day's climb.

My attitude and thought patterns could change drastically from hour to hour, leaving me wondering if I was insane. Toward the early hours of morning, I felt worry growing among us. My uncle Innocent, the strong one, was losing hope. His talk was different. He couldn't hide his troubled thoughts from us any longer. I knew if despair was settling in his heart, death was near for us. He was the rock we all needed, and I had relied on him to convince me to keep trying. I'm glad I didn't know what we'd have to endure the next day.

Hunters Overtake the Hills

On the sixth day gunshots blared through the hills like never before. The Interahamwe and the other Hutu radicals joined their power to hunt and kill Tutsis with machetes and guns. Crying babies could still be heard over the gunshots. From the trees we could see wounded Tutsi bodies quaking from the impact of the blows. Bodies were hurled through the air, falling to cruel, random graves. Whenever a Tutsi passed by, even some of the Hutu women and children shouted out their hate. Just like the militia, they joined in pitching the bodies around like dung. Not even moderate Hutus survived; to live, you had to join in killing Tutsis, or appear to be a radical.

I was seized with terror as I thought of my family. *Were they treated like they had no more worth than a manure pile?* Though I could not make out anyone's faces, my heart felt the pain of the suffering people below. The terror turned quickly to bitterness. The violence seemed unstoppable, and I slipped in and out of consciousness.

I thought about my sister Muhongayire. We were together on the first day of fleeing from our village. We ran holding hands, trying to survive the gunshots of the Interahamwe. I broke out into a dripping sweat as I recalled the heat of the firing weapons and the smothering crowds. The sound of her voice came back into my ears.

"Eric, wait for me, don't leave me all alone . . . Eric, please."

We were somehow separated as we dodged bullets. I never saw Muhongayire again. The gunfire below reminded me that

I couldn't save her. I had failed her and considered myself a coward. I have no memory of exactly when our hands slipped from each other, but I remember the crowds pushing us apart. I've tried to remember at what moment I let go of her hand, but all I can remember is the last thing she said to me:

"Wait for me, don't leave me here all alone . . ."

A Struggle to Climb

By the seventh day, I was ready to come out of hiding. I didn't care if the militia saw me or not. I was losing all desire to live.

Though my grandfather and father had talked about the reality of genocide coming again, I never thought as a young boy that I would someday be alive in this hellish existence. I thought I would have a contented life like anyone else. I had always envisioned myself thriving in my village, helping my family with the farming business and tending to the cows. But I knew this dream was now dead. I was convinced my father's family was completely exterminated and there would be no business, no legacy, to carry on as his son.

My one desire now was to die. Even though we didn't see any Interahamwe on that day, we were just waiting for the hunters to return. Eventually, to keep myself from going mad, I started to convince myself that my brothers, sisters, and mother were still alive and I would see them again. I carried on imaginary conversations with them in my head. Then I convinced myself that I too should try to survive so we could be a family again.

Though I didn't know at the time if there was a personal God or not, I believe it was at this point that God started to reveal himself to me. The voice I'd heard a few times before told me, "I've spared you from seeing more evil, so let your heart rest." I believe he sovereignly redirected the Interahamwe to pass elsewhere that day. He knew what I could bear. My uncles and I had now survived a week together. Providentially, God gave us a Sabbath from the devils in the bush on the seventh day. We went down the trees that night, but nobody was able to talk. We just rested.

More Devils in the Bush

Early into the next week, we felt a haze settle in our minds and knew we had to help one another focus. Before we climbed the trees, we determined we would all think about what life after genocide might look like. What kind of destiny would be ours if we survived? None of us had an answer, but it was our assignment for the day. We were to come up with a solution for how it might look to pursue justice for those who might survive. All of us were raised to be "serious" men. In Rwanda it's a compliment to be known as a serious man, which means you have a purpose and a plan for life.

The militia were hunting in pits and holes, big bushes and small bushes, and wherever they found Tutsis, they slaughtered them. Watching scenes of demonic power below, our hope of justice prevailing was far from our minds. We saw how every vine and thistle bush was searched by the militia. They weren't fooled by the most sharp-witted hiding place, and they followed every scrap of clothing, even if it led to just one more kill. Hutus were discovering every possible place of protection, so we knew the search was bound to turn toward the trees.

Yet we were still alive. The hunting had come to an end for that day, and our killers went back to their homes, where they gloated and bellowed their war cries against Tutsis like drunk, intoxicated demons. Though we had survived yet another battle of genocide, the deferred hope made us sick, for we knew that the next day they might look up.

Coming down for the night, we talked about a new strategy but agreed to hide in the trees yet another day. It didn't seem wise, but nothing did. There was no other alternative.

The militia groups we saw from the trees were usually grouped in hundreds. Then they would scatter into smaller groups of about forty. The hills were now infested with the stench of unimaginable evil, and the evil was only growing. Some days we sensed that the militia were growing tired; other days they seemed stronger. These men were not fighters, like admirable military men who protect. They were killers—their purpose was to murder. Their motivation was to fulfill the devil's plan to make Rwandans a divided people and ultimately wipe out a tribe. They strove to forever stain our hills with hate.

About midweek, the gunshots intensified, but I no longer feared their sound. I welcomed the guns because dying by a gunshot, I continued to reason, would be quick. The militia were close by, killing in our neighborhoods, spearing the wombs of expectant mothers, lusting to find just one more hiding place. Young and old alike were killed.

Then I heard loud gunfire in the distance . . . but it was different. The firing was much fiercer than before. Could the Interahamwe have found a way to get more weapons? Rifles. Machine guns. Other heavy guns. The shooting remained intense until sunset.

When we gathered that evening, we asked each other about the different sounds we heard. Something was different. We knew the Hutu radicals didn't have that many guns, and that they were also relying on crude handmade weapons to kill.

Uncle Innocent told us that it might be the rebels of the Rwandan Patriotic Front (RPF) trying to liberate us from the militia. We all knew about the RPF, which was organized by Rwandan refugees in Uganda. Their aim and motive for organizing was to save the people of Rwanda from future genocides. It almost pained me to cultivate a seed of hope in my heart.

We did not hear any more gunshots until around 3:00 a.m., but then we heard a growing variety of gunshots. We woke up with hope that the RPF had come to set us free. For the first time in days, we could easily justify climbing the tree another day.

The Weakening of the Enemy

This new barrage of bullets was getting closer and closer. We knew this had to mean the RPF was now seizing the Interahamwe. And from our view, we could tell the Interahamwe was no longer searching for Tutsis; rather, they killed anyone who approached them. They were aimlessly snuffing out life.

Their killing was getting sloppy, and their strategies were weakening. Satan's forces were losing control.

The shooting didn't stop until nightfall, and we continued to listen intently to discern who was in control. We also felt a great sense of relief in knowing that if we were to be murdered, the militia were now mostly using guns. But surviving now seemed like a real possibility to me.

With the hope of survival came the bleakness of facing the future. How would I start my life again without my family? I managed to listen to the voice that had been speaking to me in the trees. This voice told me it would be better to survive and that life was sacred.

When I began to believe we would indeed survive, hope filled my empty stomach. Miraculously, I no longer felt any hunger, thirst, or fatigue. I had strength to climb down the tree to sleep.

My uncles and I discussed how we didn't see groups of militia around the bushes anymore; the atmosphere was changing, which led us to believe more and more that the RPF was very close to our cluster of trees.

Over the next few days of hiding, there was no question the gunfire was now between the RPF and the Interahamwe. Some of the Interahamwe and their families started fleeing to other nearby bordering countries—Tanzania, Congo, Uganda, and Burundi. Knowing the militia were now on the run gave us the strength we needed to find refuge in the trees once again, until we knew for sure it was safe.

We began to see Hutus fleeing. As I watched them run, I imagined walking down the familiar streets of my village again. I wanted to lunge out of the tree and chase my enemy. To have the freedom to just *be* again, rather than to *be the prey* of the enemy, was a victory we could begin to experience. I felt like I was really going to make it.

After the gunfire ceased, life's battles would rage on, as we would have to face the devastation of our country. Even though our safety was now in reach, we had nowhere to go as the Interahamwe had burned down our homes, killed our cattle, and looted everything we had. I began thinking of these real obstacles that would exist when I left life in the trees.

Thoughts of my family flooded my heart. Were they still alive? I wondered if it might be possible to be happy again. Hope was growing in us all.

Liberated from Hiding

On the fourteenth morning, we saw people moving from Rwamagana to Kayonza (see the map located on page 48) and wondered whether they had been liberated by the RPF. Still we didn't get down; we stayed quietly hiding though evidence that the RPF had dominated the enemy was surrounding us. For fleeting moments throughout the day, I would even feel happy, as God's hope was trying to pry open my heart.

Because we were too far from the people who were going to Kayonza, we didn't try to follow them. We wondered how we would get accurate information about what was really happening in the surrounding villages. There was still a possibility we could be ambushed by the enemy.

We spent another day interpreting the happenings around us, and that night we all came down with lighter hearts. The end of the nightmare was near. We were almost sure we had escaped the massacre. We agreed to finally come out of hiding the next day. Gratefully we waited for the rising of the sun.

After our nightly chatter, I rested my eyes, and a flood of thoughts came to mind. I began to wonder if surviving this holocaust was really a blessing or not. Should I rejoice that my life was spared, or should I mourn as a hopeless survivor with a bleak future? Because of the violent battles of hate I had witnessed throughout my days of hiding, I was convinced that no one in my immediate family had survived. I felt the weight of being alone and the duty to carry on my family name alone.

The Last Climb

On the fifteenth day, we took our last climb just as an extra precaution. As far as our eyes could see, the surrounding hills were peaceful and quiet. Yet the silence did not erase the images of Tutsi bodies that lay below us.

My uncle Canisius heard people conversing at the side of the road. He slithered down and walked to the road and asked the cluster of people how the rest of the region was.

The smile on his face told us we could now join the rest of the survivors in Kayonza.

"You are safe again. You can come out of hiding. The RPF have covered the area," they told Canisius.

Though the news was true, it was still hard for us to believe that the militia were defeated. My eldest uncle questioned Canisius to make sure we would indeed be safe.

"How do you know we are truly safe?"

"Innocent, the people I spoke with have also been persecuted. They told me, 'The ones killing are now fleeing.'"

We didn't leave the trees right away. We waited for Uncle Innocent to determine when we would leave.

The last thing my uncles and I did under the haven of the trees was pray. Though I wasn't a Christian at the time, I knew we were talking to some God out there, as there was no way to explain our survival other than an all-powerful God watching over us. We prayed we would find our surviving relatives. We prayed for safety as we walked toward the RPF headquarters in Kayonza. Our walk would be at least twelve kilometers, so we prayed for renewed strength.

As we began this walk toward our freedom, I was gripped with the reality: *I really survived!* I turned back toward the trees and saw how beautiful they were, and I pondered how significant they had become to me. Before genocide, they graced my hills as shelter for animals, not for human life. I was beginning to believe that perhaps God planted the trees to take care of a scared, helpless sixteen-year-old boy like me. When I reached the road and could no longer see the trees, I missed them. For fifteen days of fighting off death, with little food or water, they had fed me life.

If God gave such trees a purpose on earth, I thought, *then maybe my life matters to him as well.* I later came to embrace the notion that even the radical Hutus were used as an instrument to teach me God's purpose. Somehow I knew that the Hutus didn't possess sovereignty—that belonged only to God. All of this could not be a meaningless, random happenstance. There would be more searching for me ahead in answering the questions of suffering—painful questions.

I could hardly walk, but my uncles and I fell into a comfortable pace. I was more relaxed than I could remember ever being. But now I knew I didn't have to hide my existence anymore. I wasn't afraid to walk alone, purposely straggling behind in the freedom of that day.

We joined up with more Tutsis once we reached the paved road that led away from the city of Kigali. Because of our severe physical fatigue, the walk took most of the day.

As we walked toward the RPF, we had more time to talk freely about how we had escaped. I caught up with Canisius to ask him the details of his story. I wanted to know what had happened to him and how he had made it to the trees.

Canisius

Running from My Neighbors

Your path led through the sea, your way through the mighty waters, though your footprints were not seen.

Psalm 77:19

Ruyombyana Canisius is a man I am proud to call Uncle. Though he is not a big man physically, his strength and wit allowed him to overcome the bleak odds of survival. When I first heard his personal story of escape, I had no doubt that God was more powerfully present than the devil allowed us to know. When Canisius first told me how he survived, I could only shout at him, "You by all accounts should be dead. You're a miracle!"

Very few of my family members lived through the hillside massacre. Those who did were scattered and vulnerable to attack, but miraculously Canisius was still with his older brother and they ran together toward the neighboring vil-

69

lage where they had hoped to rest. Before dark they found a sandpit that was used to make bricks for houses. They slept there for the night.

Friends and Enemies

The morning after the massacre, Canisius saw a Hutu killer chasing a woman and her baby boy out of a pit. The Interahamwe had discovered their hiding place. So Canisius and his brother knew that holes and pits were not safe for long. Their only option was to begin running again, and they had to separate.

Canisius was able to keep pace with his neighbor, Rwigamba Jen Bosco. They fled together for a long distance, running seven or eight miles without stopping. When they finally stopped in a nearby neighborhood he was familiar with, Canisius could not believe his eyes. He told me later with hot tears, "My Hutu neighbors were killing my cousins, my friends. The enemies who surrounded us had been my neighbors just days ago—my friends whom I loved."

They stopped to hide in the bush and choked down their disbelief at seeing Canisius's Hutu neighbors returning from killing our family members. One other Tutsi who had been hiding in the bush nearby suddenly ran out in the open, thinking he had spotted his brother among the crowd. But it was a Hutu man wearing his brother's clothes. As he approached the group, he found they were militia, but he also recognized them from our village. Horrified, the Tutsi boy ran back. Rwigamba was certain their Hutu neighbors wouldn't kill them because of the close friendship they'd had just days ago.

The Hutu killers found them and grabbed Canisius by his jacket. Soon the whole mob was grabbing him, ripping off his clothes.

"Spare me, please. You know me . . . I know you . . . please, don't kill," he pleaded. "We just shared our food together the other day."

The Hutus showed no mercy in their hateful response: "We know we have shared food and drink. We know that we know you. We don't care that we grew up as friends. We just want to exterminate all Tutsis."

The mob became more violent and began to beat my uncle. Their ruthless banter went back and forth: "How shall we kill him? With a machete? A sword?"

Canisius yelled out, "Please, I'm going to just lie down. Just kill me straight away!"

A Merciful Neighbor

The leader of this group was a man named Rutinkduka Etienne. He was a family friend to all of us and like an uncle to us as we grew up. Etienne had even taught Canisius how to ride a bicycle. He had often visited their house to play with my uncle. He approached the men surrounding Canisius, not knowing at first that it was him. When he realized who his men were beating, he commanded, "Stop it!"

I believe God must have touched his heart at that moment. As the leader of the group, he was risking his reputation in suggesting they spare the life of a Tutsi. And Etienne had already shown Canisius mercy the day genocide broke out, before this violent night. Even before we left our homes, he had warned my uncle that the Interahamwe was plotting to kill us all.

"Men, you listen to me," he said to the crowd. "Canisius is a very close friend of my family. Spare his life. He is their only family member still alive. No doubt he will be killed later, but not by us. If any of you kill him, I will kill you myself!" threatened Etienne.

Miraculously, the mob listened to their leader, and my uncle's life was spared. Etienne took Canisius to a mango tree and told him to hide there.

"I know you will be killed, but you will not be killed in front of me. May God protect you. Just stay here. The tree will give you an opportunity to live."

That night Canisius came down from the tree to see if Rwigamba was still alive. He was still breathing just a little bit. His wounds were many: on his head, neck, chest, and legs. His handsome face was swollen and severely bludgeoned. Canisius wondered how he could find water for him. As he stood there, the killers spotted him. He began to run again, back toward the hill they had come from, Nyarusange. He ran back because his mother's brother lived on this hill and had a large farm. As he made yet another escape, he saw bodies in the dark bushes and bodies scattered in the road; he had to stumble over death. Children hiding in the bushes were sobbing quietly, but Canisius knew that he could not let their cries paralyze him if he were to survive. He began to pray that

God would send a soldier with a machete to kill him. He told me, "I wasn't running because I thought I would live. I was running with the motivation of wanting to meet my killer."

When Canisius reached the farm, his uncle Munyinya took him in to hide. Munyinya whispered, "Your two brothers are here too."

When Canisius's brothers saw him enter the barn, they began to cry, "We were told you were killed." They all hid under bales of hay.

After a while when you find yourself running alone, you begin to believe there are no other Tutsi survivors but you. Encouraged by being with his family, Canisius stayed one night in our uncle's barn. There were rumors the killers were specifically after my uncle.

Before daybreak the four of them left the barn and ran back to hide in the bush. There they stayed two days. It began to rain, and they came out of hiding to stretch and walk about a bit. When the rain passed, they went back into hiding. But they had left their footprints, and the killers tracked them down. They spotted Canisius's younger brother but not the other three.

"Iyenzi [cockroach], are you alone?" they demanded to know.

"Yes, I am alone."

The Hutus took him away and killed him back in the village. To keep count of all the Tutsis who died and report back to their leaders, the killers would try to take their victims to where they were from. As a part of their routine, later they returned to see if there was another to slaughter. That's when they found Canisius and his two brothers.

The Hutus stripped the three who were left to see if they had any money; one of them had 70 francs. The Hutus led my cousins back to their neighborhood and gave them their clothes. They continued to brutally beat them as they passed through a valley, leading them to their abandoned homes. Then one of the militia saw armed soldiers fleeing on the other side of the hill. They were confused and thought the soldiers were RPF soldiers—so the militia ran. These three Tutsis, my courageous uncles, escaped once again.

Canisius and his brothers ran back to the farm to hide again. My great-uncle was there and instructed them, "Climb into the trees. The Interahamwe are not wise enough to check the trees. They know to check pits and holes but not trees." So they climbed into the row of cypress trees. It was almost 3:00 a.m. My uncles wouldn't know until morning that my path of escape led me right to them.

Mugabo

Fleeing from the Devil

See how the faithful city has become a harlot! She once was full of justice; righteousness used to dwell in her—but now murderers!

Isaiah 1:21

Mugabo Egide is my brother and my hero. Like my uncle Canisius, he is a walking miracle. Many times he had to look the enemy in the eye and determine with every fiber of his soul that he was resolved to escape. Throughout the genocide, I was uncertain of his whereabouts or if he was still alive. His personal account of survival shouts out to me, "There is a God!" and I believe hosts of heavenly armies looked after him, guiding his every step so that he might live to tell his powerful testimony.

Family groups were formed by my grandfather and my uncles. Women and small children were instructed to find safety in nearby shelters. Mugabo was not big enough to flee with the group I was in. A few days after genocide broke out, around April 12, he was taken to the mayor's office to hide. There he found our mother, as they had been separated for a few days. My family thought the government would protect them there. But in reality people were being killed everywhere—hospitals, churches, schools, and government buildings. When they arrived on a Wednesday, the killers were on the loose not too far away. By Friday they came to kill.

Many people who fled to this site were women with their children—around fifteen thousand. Mugabo could see the hunters coming over the next hill in trucks. He knew there was no way to fight them without any weapons. Survival meant running.

The militia started shooting around 1:00 p.m., and the Tutsis were all surrounded. Most of our family was sitting around the government compound, but Mugabo ran behind it and hid in a hole that was dug for future construction. The shooting stopped after a few hours, and he came out of hiding, thinking the stilled air meant it was safe to climb out. He saw Tutsis were gathering all the stones and bricks they could to throw, trying to stay alive, but they were not able to overpower the militia's weapons.

When Mugabo stepped out from behind the compound, an Interahamwe soldier saw him and threw a grenade. He dodged behind an isombe tree. Shrapnel flew, hitting his leg, but the tree protected him from a fatal blow. A Hutu man called out to him, gloating, "All of your family has been killed." Because the killers oftentimes knew families personally from their neighborhoods, they would try to break their victims down emotionally by claiming their family members had been killed.

The crazed sounds of war made my little brother dizzy and faint. He couldn't stand to hear the cows bleating out, looking for their mothers. He wanted to rescue them. But he knew he had to shut them out of his mind; he had to keep going.

He later told me, "I ran back to where I last saw my mother, as any young boy would seek refuge in his mother's arms. I saw her lying on the steps bleeding and limp. She had been shot. My four-year-old brother, Mahungu Murindwa, was still on her back. He cried out to me, 'Muga.'"

Mugabo ran quickly toward little Mahungu and pulled him out of the sling so he could hold him in his arms. In horror, Mugabo realized that the bullet that shot his mother had penetrated into his baby brother's face, slicing off his nose and cheek. Mugabo tried to collect extra clothing to shelter the bodies of those shot on the steps of the government building. Time was short and he knew he had to be quick. Mahungu was profusely bleeding in his arms.

Eight thousand were killed at this government compound, a massacre known as Gishari Akarere Ka Rwamagana.

Those who survived became instant soldiers—even the children. My family had a meeting, and some of my uncles broke into the police building to grab guns to protect the group. They walked together for about five miles, looking to see if there were any signs of the RPF coming to stop the outbreak. Mugabo kept walking in a state of shock, stroking Mahungu's bloody face. He kept walking, hoping to find an answer, a strategy that would save them. Mugabo later stumbled through tears as he remembered:

> I must have walked about twenty miles before coming to Muhazi Lake, where others were gathered. We had to hike over four hills before we came to the shore. After the second hill, I noticed Mahungu had stopped breathing. We were in a bushy part of the forest, and with no other choice, I took him off my back and laid him in a soft place where his body would not be noticed. In my anguish I just wanted to stay with him.
>
> We had the guns that we took with us from the police building. The militia who were also at the lake only had machetes. We knew we were more powerful and would be able to defend ourselves.
>
> We needed to cross the very large Muhazi Lake, but there was only one boat that could transport only six people at a time—there were four thousand of us. Out of desperation some were just jumping in, trying to swim across. Tutsis crossed in shifts with this one feeble boat from about 9:00 p.m. to 2:00 a.m. Those who did not make it across before dawn were killed.

Those who crossed were able to run ahead to the zone occupied by the RPF—the only hope of protection. Those who were still waiting for the boat stayed until daybreak. About that time, two Hutu children came to fetch water. After these children saw the crowd Mugabo was in, they motioned to the militia that a group of Tutsis was still there. My brother didn't know the people around him anymore, except one teacher he recognized from school.

The Tutsis knew they had to move. The elders in this crowd instructed my brother to move away from the lakeside to the hills, though he was aware he would be confronted by militia along the way.

The militia knew crowds had fled to the lake. They knew about those who fled from the government building. As the small number of survivors saw their killers approaching them, they knew the enemy outnumbered them. Soon the militia overtook the Tutsis who were left.

Not many survived this battle. Some Tutsi people still had guns, so they continued to defend the weak and the younger as long as they could. Gradually the militia was also weakening, and soon they just stopped trying to kill and retreated.

Some survivors were still trying to run from the killers but were too weak. Those without guns pelted stones at their predators in hopes of pulling one more step away from death. Others threw themselves in the lake to drown so that they wouldn't die at the hands of the militia.

The hills were wild with fiery hatred as the machete blows decapitated innocent people. Some of the militia had been joined now by Hutu civilians. You could identify them by their headdresses made of grass.

Mugabo was in the midst of killers, running without direction. He told me, "I turned and saw a head slashed off a man right in front of my eyes. The head fell down the hill, away from the decapitated body. Anger welled up inside me, more anger than I thought I was capable of, as the killer spotted me after slaying his victim. I ran with all my might, and he saw he could not catch me. The killer flung something, possibly a dismembered body part, but I just kept running. My foot was wounded pretty seriously at some point. . . . Then I ran alone."

After a while Mugabo came across four other survivors. He spotted them running together alongside the river. The militia also spotted them. Three of the Tutsis went down and hid in the marsh. My brother quickly found a banana plant close to the marsh not far from them. One man was separated from the others and fled down the road. He kept running but soon was killed by a Hutu with a machete.

The Hutus noticed Mugabo close by where the man was killed.

"You look like a dog," the Hutu killer cursed at my brother.

Mugabo is not sure what stopped the man from pressing the machete against his flesh, but he did not kill Mugabo. The Hutus confronted the other man who was hiding nearby. They checked the victim's pockets and found 35,000 Rwandan francs, which is about $200. They took the money and killed him. Mugabo was left alone, still hiding beside the banana tree.

Four thousand more lives were lost at the lakeside massacre. I still cannot fathom how my young brother was one of three survivors.

A Sacred Leaf

Mugabo stayed in the banana tree all the next morning. Right before he came out, he overheard a group of Hutus talking with an old man.

"Why didn't you carry a sorghum leaf for protection?" he screamed at the Hutu crowd. "We must all be careful to only kill Tutsi."

My brother realized this was a secret sign Hutus used to declare their identity to one another as a means of protection. So he quickly picked a sorghum leaf from a plant nearby and took it with him.

Carrying his sorghum leaf, he left the bush and came across a man who was plundering an abandoned Tutsi house. He was trying to get a cupboard out when he saw Mugabo.

"Come help me put this on my head."

Mugabo helped him carry the cupboard a ways before the man looked at him and began to question him.

"Who are you? Aren't you Tutsi?"

"No sir, I am not Tutsi," Mugabo asserted, clutching the leaf to his chest.

"Then where are you from?"

Fumbling, he said, "I am from the other side of the hill."

Grabbing his machete, the man shouted, "Then you are Tutsi!"

From out of nowhere an old woman screamed, "Don't kill that child! I beg you, do not kill him."

The man kicked Mugabo and said, "Go away, you dog," then kept on walking.

Mugabo came to Ruhunda, a village he did not know, so he just kept walking to keep moving. He saw another crowd of militia who had just killed a cow for meat. They were noisy and wild.

Mugabo yelped in fright as he saw their glaring eyes quickly turn toward him. Three of them began to chase him. Quickly he ran toward the house ahead, which belonged to one of the men chasing him. Mugabo ran through the front gates.

In the Rwandan culture, if an animal that is being hunted happens to make it into the compound of a house, it is considered unethical to kill it. It's customarily believed that when you protect the hunted prey after it has entered your gates, it's a blessing to your home.

"You don't have to kill the child; he has entered the compound," shouted a Hutu man from inside.

Though Mugabo's life was cruelly compared to an animal, his life once again was spared to honor a superstitious belief.

That night this Hutu family gave him food. They fed him bananas and meat arranged on a leaf. He later told me, "I had seen the militia kill the cow with the machete which now was used to cut my dinner meat. Nausea filled my stomach, and I could not consume anything. They put me outside to eat, and I decided to flee once again."

On the run for quite some time, Mugabo came across another Tutsi child. When the child saw Mugabo, he became scared, but my brother told him, "Don't worry, we will run together."

The young boy told him some of his story and said the hills he had climbed were too numerous to count. They decided to stick together.

As the two boys moved over the hills, they were confronted by a very angry man with a machete. But his mother and sister saw he wanted to harm them, so they took hold of the Hutu man and shook him away from the boys. There was no way to tell who would protect and who would kill.

Mugabo ran one way; the other Tutsi boy ran the other way. The big man followed the trail of the other boy.

"I kept running until I reached a main dirt road," Mugabo recounted. "I wanted to move ahead and get to a place that was familiar. It was here I came across a big number of Interahamwe. They were just sitting together, drinking beer."

"Who are you? What are you doing here?" shouted one man. "Do you think you are going to escape from us?"

Another man raised his sword at Mugabo, questioning again, "Who are you? Tell me the truth!"

"I'm from the other side of the hill," he told them. "I was trying to flee from people who were trying to kill us, but I'm not scared. I'm just not scared."

"Who is your family, boy? Are you Tutsi?"

"No, I am not Tutsi. I am from a Hutu family," Mugabo asserted. "One of my friends is Tutsi, but after I knew what was happening I decided to go back to my house so I could get away." He paused for their reaction and swallowed hard, still carrying his sorghum leaf.

"Well then, you are a courageous man. . . . Go ahead."

Mugabo went on his way until he came across a roadblock of about thirty people. They were Hutu children, probably between the ages of ten and fifteen, who were also participating in genocide. They looked intently at Mugabo's physical appearance. They examined the lines on his hands as if a Hutu hand would be different than a Tutsi's, though in reality there were not enough physical differences between the tribes. One could be mistakenly slaughtered or spared on the whim of the militia.

"I'm Hutu." Mugabo looked down and saw the sticks and stones they had gathered to kill other Tutsi children.

"Okay, let him go. Leave him alone," yelled the crazed leader.

After yet another close escape, Mugabo headed to a house nearby that had a compound. A young man inside jumped over the compound wall toward him before he could enter the gates. He threw Mugabo down and stepped on his stomach. The killer drew his sword and pressed it against Mugabo's neck.

A man came running toward Mugabo, shouting, "Leave that child alone. I know him." Mugabo realized this man had been at the lakeside massacre. He had killed many people and still had blood on his clothes. Yet, strangely, he said to spare Mugabo's life. Mugabo didn't understand this. God seemed to be thwarting the plans of all predators in his path.

This Hutu man who saved Mugabo's life took Mugabo to his own house. On the way they came across another young Tutsi child, who quickly tried to escape. The man stopped in the middle of the road and killed this child in front of my brother. Mugabo was paralyzed with fear. He could do nothing but try to stand firm and not let his knees give way.

"Somehow I managed to move my feet as the Hutu man steered me to his home," Mugabo later told me. "He kept me outside of his house but brought me food—meat and potatoes. I still had no appetite from seeing the cow slaughtered earlier, so I threw it over my shoulder. He came to check on me and said, 'Look at you, you ate all of this food! You must have been so hungry.'

"I soon learned this man was uncertain of my identity, so he kept bringing other militia to scrutinize my identity. Somehow I was able to convince them. I stayed there Saturday, Sunday, Monday, Tuesday. On that Wednesday the RPF was starting to take over. That day he also brought another Hutu from the northern part of the country."

The Hutu man said, "I've checked him out—he's Tutsi."

"No, no! I'm Hutu," Mugabo cried.

Mugabo told me, "The man of this house was wild with hate. I knew he was emotionally disturbed from his own acts of murder. His clothes had layers of blood stains, so I knew he was still hunting others every day. But I learned his wife was a Tutsi. There were two children. This family was made up of very strong, forceful men, and all were supporters of the militia. Because of their physical strength, they were able to protect the Tutsi wife. But soon I could no longer pass their interrogation."

Mugabo was going to be killed on Thursday. He woke up very early and escaped once again, heading back to our village. He knew there might be a chance to live if he were able to just get back to Rwamagana.

The Last Escape

At early dawn, he could see people along the way who were fleeing—they were militia. He hid in the bush until they passed.

"I felt my heart strengthening as more and more militia were fleeing around the borders of my village," Mugabo told me. "The sun was barely shedding light over the trees, but I could still see. . . . I was shocked to see that my village was covered with the RPF. The militia had fled. I was now safe."

Mugabo ran to the hospital because he knew there would be RPF there to help. He stayed there until Sunday. Some killing was still taking place, but he knew he had enough protection.

By Sunday all the people who survived and arrived in Rwamagana were safe. The RPF was strong enough to cover this area completely. In the course of these days, life felt void of movement for Mugabo—he didn't feel anything. He couldn't speak. All around him he heard others share their stories of survival. But he couldn't relive or speak of his own.

For two months my brother remained in an orphanage and felt the comfort of the other children around him, though he wouldn't communicate or talk with anyone. He showed no emotions and pulled himself inward to his own world. He was existing in emptiness, trying to forget and reject what his eyes had witnessed.

As a young man now, like all who survived, Mugabo can't fully make sense of the genocide. But when he shares his testimony, his words are honest and help me better make sense of it all.

Mugabo says, "Maybe part of the reason I'm here is to tell the world good can really happen in any life. You know, I think of the lakeside massacre and how only three of us survived out of thousands. . . . There is a responsibility I feel in that. I don't believe my life was spared because I was better than those perished. But I have to trust God's mysterious plan that I was chosen to survive. When I was in the hole, hiding at the government compound, I remember saying to God, 'If you keep me alive, I will serve you all of my life.' And when I was dodging the devils in the bush, I cried out, 'God, if you save me, I shall serve you all of my life.'"

After Mugabo gave his life to Christ, a genocide song came to be his strong reminder of how God answered him in the bush and of the promise he made to God. Not too many years ago, he was working in the street where he heard a small boy singing this song:

> When you were trying to hide yourself in the bush,
> you promised God you would serve him day and
> night,
> and today you're failing God and you're failing the
> covenant . . .
> God saved you; remember the covenant you made . . .

Instantly his mind took him back to the bush. He recalled everything, and he remembered the covenant he made with God. That was a turning point in his walk. Mugabo knows without a shadow of a doubt that God went to great lengths to keep him alive through escape after escape.

Postlude

The many miracles of escape through which Canisius, Mugabo, and I survived leave us humbled. We don't know all the reasons our lives were spared, but we know it is not because we were more worthy than others who did not survive the genocide. Because God is love, we can trust his sovereignty.

I know God led Canisius to find the shelter of the mango tree. I know God led Mugabo to find protection from a sorghum leaf. Without a doubt, I know the cypress trees were sovereignly planted to spare the lives of my uncles and me.

Our stories of survival are a mystery and a grace; we know God wanted to bring us back together for a greater good we have yet to fully understand. Our story has brought us closer together as family and closer to almighty God. We know God is the author of our story.

> And he shall be like a tree planted by the rivers of water, that bringeth forth his fruit in his season; his leaf also shall not wither; and whatsoever he doeth shall prosper.
>
> Psalm 1:3 KJV

PART 3
The Will to Survive

Searching for Family

For where two or three gather together as my followers, I am
there among them.

Matthew 18:20 NLT

When my uncles and I finally arrived in Kayonza, all we
wanted to do was search for family members, so we scattered around the village. We heard so many stories of survival
that left us stunned.

Did this really happen, and how did we ever survive? We
had not eaten in over fifteen days, and our appetites had
subsided. We had to relearn how to desire food to gain our
strength.

Clusters of Tutsis stood in the streets, taking in the devastation of the surrounding villages in disbelief. The wreckage
made it almost impossible to see a future. We felt like Ezekiel
walking into the valley of dry bones. The stench of death.
Demolished homes. Rancid food. Broken families. How could

life be brought back to all the neighboring villages? We had to convince ourselves we all were alive for a reason.

Everyone was asking questions about their family members. *When was the last time you saw my brother? Does anyone know if my mother survived? Did anyone see my baby?* Though we had to face stories of terror through these days, we felt safe knowing the RPF were in control of the area. No longer did we have to silence what we had witnessed.

After I gained enough strength, I decided to go to Rwamagana to look for family members. For many days I went back and forth, asking survivors if they had seen any of my family. The RPF saw me trek over the hills every day and took a liking to me. One of my uncles was a leader on the force, and sometimes the soldiers would go with me on my journey. I think they liked my resolve to find my family and wanted to encourage me to keep trying. The soldiers even let me work with them, which gave me something meaningful to do. We knew the RPF's goal was for every Rwandan to be able to live peacefully with one another again. With their help, I searched and searched for my family with constant pangs of worry in my heart.

The soldiers would ask, "Eric, what can I do for you? Can we help you find your family and go with you to your village?" My father used to ask me that too: "Son, what can I do for you?"

I felt very comfortable with them, and I liked how safe I felt in their company. Their skill fascinated me. I continued to seek out their companionship throughout the weeks ahead while some of my friends and relatives continued to gather and come out from hiding.

My Reunion with Mugabo

I don't know exactly how long it took me to find my brother Mugabo. Mugabo remembers some details that I cannot recall. Though our timelines of the genocide are blurry, I remember vividly the moment of our reunion, as does Mugabo.

"After seeing Eric," Mugabo recounted, "I felt shocked back into life. I couldn't speak or tell my big brother that I was so happy he was alive—genocide left me mute.

"The RPF had taken care of me for about two months at an orphanage. I didn't play with the other orphans. I was very depressed and became very detached from the life around me. Mostly I just remember sitting alone with my sad thoughts. But when I saw Eric, I had the instant impulse to run to him. He held me a long time and his flood of tears warmed my back. My emotions were still far away, but in the days ahead Eric helped bring them back to me."

It is hard to communicate exactly how I felt to find Mugabo alive. Were we really supposed to be the remnant of our family? Could we even survive another day in a dead country? How would I ever be able to give him a good life? I felt like my chest was about to explode as I laid eyes on him after months of searching. His eyes had lost their spark, and I tried not to be alarmed at his skeletal frame. I closed my eyes and we embraced silently. I knew his survival story had to be full of miracles. I wanted to know everything, but we didn't talk. We just sat together, amazed.

Having one another kept us going in the coming months. Life had to start over for us, but with no means or resources. I was still so young and just beginning to realize the daunting

95

responsibility of caring for my brother. I was now his parent but with no home to offer him.

In the weeks ahead, all of my surviving family members exchanged intense stories, and we needed to listen to one another out of respect. But there were days when I just couldn't listen anymore. Reliving the genocide made it hard to move forward. I became physically ill and fatigued when I heard a testimony of escape. But none of us knew Mugabo's story yet. I hoped with each passing day to hear his voice again.

I wouldn't know for some time how courageous my little brother really was. I could only speculate what his innocent eyes had seen. I had to fight off depression as people continued to reunite and also mourn when they were told a loved one was confirmed to be dead. Though families were coming together, we didn't seem to have enough life in us to keep going. There was too much loss to face.

More were now returning from other bordering countries. When some Rwandan refugee families returned, they could not believe that Tutsi children had survived. They immediately assumed we had to be children of the Interahamwe.

Strengthened by Love

In the trying days that followed, Mugabo and I gave each other strength. Mugabo could not speak at first, but our communication went far beyond words. Many days I wished I did not have to wake up again. Yet God was imparting his plan for my life, though at the time I only saw shattered lives.

Mugabo recounts:

Over the course of several weeks, Eric showered me with love and talked with me each day. The comfort of his voice was planting hope back into my heart. I wanted to speak and tell him everything. Yet my mind was still telling me the physical world around me was not safe. But each day I found myself moving more toward the edges of reality, where Eric and all the other survivors were. I did not speak after the genocide for about two years. Then one day I saw my friend Patrick. I didn't know he was alive.

"Patrick!" I cried out, though I remember it wasn't easy to stutter out his name.

As I tried to continue to talk, emotions were fighting their way back into my heart. It was so difficult to let go of my safe, empty world. But I kept fighting my way out. Slowly, I could speak again.

My spirits lifted and my overall outlook changed when Mugabo began to speak. I knew he was a fighter and a strong boy, but I also knew he had lived through the vilest of days. Not knowing fully what he saw firsthand, I was unsure if he would ever speak of it or be able to tell me what had happened.

For a time, the genocide robbed Mugabo of all passion for life. It was so hard for his heart to move past the pain. No one expected him to just move on, but I knew that if he kept trying, he could speak again. Our bond as brothers continued to be strengthened and I assured him, "I will not leave you alone. We are safe now."

Even once he could speak again, Mugabo was still profoundly traumatized. I couldn't take away all his pain, but I knew personally how the presence of another human being brings healing. We'd sit and talk things out, just trying to cope with the shredded-up lives we were left with.

I'm always amazed to hear how much Mugabo remembers:

Around the time I started to speak again, Eric became a Christian. He was now attending Restoration Church and sharing with me the hope God was bringing into his own life.

"Muga," he would say to me, "did you know the Bible says God is the Father to the orphans and the widows?" He continued to read me more of God's promises, repeating over and over that God was our Father. He kept trying to assure me that if we would just move on with God from this place, he would show us his plan. Eric showed me this Scripture:

Remember your Creator in the days of your youth, before the days of trouble come and the years approach when you will say, "I find no pleasure in them"—before the sun and the light and the moon and the stars grow dark, and the clouds return after the rain; when the keepers of the house tremble, and the strong men stoop, when the grinders cease because they are few, and those looking through the windows grow dim. (Eccles. 12:1–3)

Though I was ten years old, the genocide left me like an old man who had endured many wars of evil. I felt like a soldier who had never been relieved from battle. Everything looked different to me after the war, broken and empty. But I knew what Eric was telling me about God must be true. I had to forget the madness and move toward this Creator God he was telling me about. I knew Eric was telling me the truth, but the climb toward God seemed like another long journey, and I didn't know if I had the strength to follow. It was a long process for me. Slowly I was beginning to believe this God could give me back my youth.

Later Mugabo moved to an orphanage started by French missionaries, called Friends of Children, for about four years. This was a stable home for him where he had loving houseparents who shared their faith with all the children. The economy was still bad, so I couldn't afford a house. Mugabo's closest friends today are those he grew up with at the orphanage.

A Boy Called Mugabo Egide

Though my brother would tell you that I was the one to inspire him to keep on living, he had no idea how I was leaning on him at the time. He gave me a focus beyond myself. I still struggle with anger at how the genocide robbed him of his childhood, but he acknowledges that with God's help, he isn't afraid to confront his pain. And I admit, he has dealt with his trauma much more openly than I have.

When Mugabo was in the orphanage, I was working most of the time. He felt misplaced and abandoned, like he was waiting to die. Today he comes with me to visit the orphans, because he knows how the presence of another human being mysteriously strengthens them to keep trying. He tells me, "I don't feel alone anymore, and I feel like I need to be close to the orphans and show them they are not alone. . . . I would like to have an orphanage and take in homeless children who are emotionally wounded and place them in an atmosphere of love. . . . I've learned it is possible to more than just survive. . . . Life can let you live again. He [God] is teaching me more than I thought was possible to know in one lifetime."

Mugabo's dream to work in ministry with orphans is already happening. He volunteers his time with me and brings so much laughter to our gatherings—a much-needed, God-given medicine. His dream is to build a Christian orphanage in every district of the country.

Mugabo is thriving now, and I know he will be a great father someday. He currently works as a freelance photographer and has a small co-op construction business called Chez Mugabo.

Finding Murinzi Daniel

My own search for more of my siblings continued, and another miracle happened—Daniel, my six-year-old brother, was alive! He had been placed in a different orphanage than Mugabo.

My aunt, Mukamana Esperence, saved Murinzi Daniel's life. As her own flight from the genocide began, she had the very hard responsibility of trying to keep the children safe. She does not speak of her experience in great detail due to the trauma. The tears flowed as she recalled, "I had my own children, my sister's child, and Daniel. We had to start fleeing on April 14. [It was] very hard to hide the children, but we first found shelter in the bushes."

My aunt knew that the bushes would not be a safe place for long, as the militia continued to ransack their way through the villages and hills. She heard the militia coming and ran to a nearby house for safety. But by the next morning, the house owner, who was Hutu, knew it would cause him trouble to hide them. Some Hutus were hiding Tutsis, especially clergy, and the Interahamwe would kill anyone who was assisting a "cockroach."

The only weapon Esperence had was her maternal instincts. She ran with the children to a marsh and used the covering of the brush. Others were hiding there. The militia was on the other side and shooting toward them. But they didn't run; they were all quiet until dark.

Again my aunt tried to find a house for the sake of the children. Her own baby girl was only eight months old and needed nourishment. Esperence knocked on the houses of Hutu people whom she had known just days before as friends, but she couldn't find a family who would take in even one child. Finally the fourth house she tried did take them in. She said, "There we slept one night. In the morning we heard the noise of attacks. The Hutu house owner let us go."

Early that morning, Auntie was forced to try to survive in the bush. She could not run fast with the children. They managed to go unnoticed for three days in one spot. She recalled, "All I can remember was telling the children, 'Stand still and keep quiet. People are chasing us and want to kill us.' . . . The daytime was particularly hard for the children to remain quiet and still. I don't remember which child said this, but later in the afternoon one said, 'This is worse than being killed. Let's go find someone who will just kill us!' I had few words of comfort as I knew my baby severely needed nourishment and had not eaten at this point for three days."

In desperation, my aunt gathered the children and fled aimlessly. They came to a big road and found that no one was there. They crossed the road and she found a man she knew named Clement. Esperence was friends with this man's daughter.

At first she thought Clement might chase them away because he was from a Hutu family, but he didn't. Auntie and the children stayed there, and the family helped them dig a hole to hide in. They put a cover over it through which they could breathe. At night they could get out of the hole and sleep. She told me, "I wasn't living a life where I was mindful of the days at all, but we were there in the hole hiding for probably about a week or more. Soon we were hearing others talk about safety and that the RPF were coming. We stayed there until they came."

One family came to tell them to go where the RPF had thoroughly covered the area. As soon as she was sure, Auntie traveled about three miles with the young children. Sadly, my cousin, baby Ishimwe Lillian, died from living in the hole. The trauma of that night still hovers over Auntie Esperence when she remembers.

As they reached safety, the RPF took them in and provided food and shelter at a camp. From here the survivors were asked by the government to tour the remaining Hutu houses in order to find places to live because most of the Tutsi homes were destroyed. Here my aunt had food, shelter, and everything she needed. Murinzi Daniel was taken to an orphanage.

My aunt knew he was at least safe. I found him about four months after Mugabo and I were reunited.

Daniel was the only other surviving sibling I would find throughout long months of searching, waiting, and disappointment. Joyful moments could very quickly turn to sorrow. One minute I was grieving over the death of a friend or cousin, and the next I was marveling at the dignity of another's courage to survive, miraculously escaping this evil raid on humanity.

Murinzi Daniel is now twenty-two years old, handsome and much taller than me. He is growing into a strong man with many friends. Daniel has accepted Christ as his Savior, so I know his future is secure. Though he has no recollection of genocide, he fully knows what it is like to live in the wake of its devastation.

Searching for a Better Life

Before the genocide, our village was a gathering place for both Tutsi and Hutu. The pre-genocide culture was to share everything freely with our neighbors. When there was a wedding in our village, all the neighbors and the whole village would bring food and drinks, regardless of their tribal identity. Or if there was a death in a family, people came from very far away to pay respect and encourage the family. All Rwandans are trying to find the way back to such gatherings. It's happening, but slowly.

My brothers and I have come a long way. We've had to redefine what family life should be like and what really matters. I am still maturing and growing myself. God has been patient with me. We still mourn the loss of our father, mother, brother, sisters, and countless other relatives. I think about how my parents are now a part of the great cloud of witnesses and must marvel at God's grace in my life, in Mugabo's life, and in Daniel's life. They know we are children of God now, safe because we know what it means to gather in his name, no matter where we find ourselves.

A Life Resurrected

Never be afraid to trust an unknown future to a known God.

Corrie ten Boom

After the genocide the new government under the arm of the RPF was faced with staggering conditions. The whole country was in upheaval. An estimated one million people were murdered in roughly one hundred days. Some Hutus escaped, but all the Hutu refugees were being asked to return to Rwanda and face their crimes. Those who came to confess their sin of genocide received a reduced sentence in prison. Rwandans had no idea how justice could ever be served.

Tutsis made up almost 15 percent of the population before genocide; an estimated 77 percent of them were slaughtered. The death toll of over a million was the most killed per day in any war of history to date. The kinds of sufferings survivors had to face daily were wide and vast. Children were orphaned, spouses were widowed, and the brutal effects of poverty were overwhelming. There was not enough medical aid to tend to the sick, nor was there counseling available to help with our hidden, internal wounds. For months there was no local police force and no court system to convict killers who were still in Rwanda. The monetary system had crashed, and there was no cash. About 1.2 million Hutus were said to have fled from the country, and many Tutsis were still frightened. Reclaiming our land among the devastation was going to take time and resources our country didn't have.

My brothers and I stayed alive with governmental help for almost two years. Most days it was hard to believe in our future. Yet I kept searching for opportunities to work and trying to find a way to pay for Mugabo's and Daniel's education. Due to the genocide, I would not be able to go on to university, but I was determined to send my brothers.

We faced long, hard months with no tangible signs of progress. Rebuilding our country was going to take years. But in 1996, opportunities to work began to surface. Finally my mind was occupied with something other than the devastation of my country. I could now focus on bettering myself for my family. I felt a level of sanity return as we began to hear rumors of job opportunities. My uncles who survived also did all they could to help me and my brothers.

No matter what I was doing with my brothers, I felt the need to instill hope in their lives and cast a vision for our surviving family. I concealed my doubts and worry as much as I could, hoping they would never suspect my own despair. After months that turned into over a year, my brothers left the orphanage to live with other surviving family members for a time, but we still saw each other as much as possible. We knew the importance of sticking together.

Government and private programs were working to help survivors make a new start. I heard about an opportunity to attend a trade school for mechanics in Kigali and decided to sign up. Deciding to relocate to the city and leave my brothers was tough, but I knew it would be better for them in the long run if I learned a skill. I studied from 7:30 a.m. to 5:00 p.m. during the week and would head back to Rwamagana on the weekends. My mind felt alive again as I began studying and getting under the hood of a car to apply my new skills. The supervisor of the program was pleased with my performance and offered me remuneration on the side to gain experience fixing cars. Though I was still homeless, my wages continued to increase, and I was able to help support my family.

A New Kind of Hope

One evening on my way back home from a holiday break, I passed by an open area in Rwamagana and heard praying. I looked around at the people, some sitting in the grass, others sitting in makeshift pews, listening to the pastor. I decided to go sit down for a moment before heading to see my family. Hanging above the platform was a banner that read "Restoration Church, Pastor Gasore Constantin, Preaching words of hope to genocide survivors." The church was fasting for forty days and having nightly prayer gatherings. Sitting there on a pew, I held my head down, not wanting to be noticed. I didn't want any part of church or God; I had become so disillusioned with God in the months following the genocide. I could not fathom a God who would allow everything to be taken from me and my family. The only reason I stopped there was because I wanted to be surrounded by other survivors so I wouldn't feel so lonely.

The pastor's words were drowned out by noise in my head. I was wondering about my life and future—unsure if I was really going to make it. I wasn't really aware of anyone but myself that night; I didn't care about the sermon or what others were praying about. I actually thought that the people gathered were foolish to even try to pray. *The God of the Bible does not really exist*, I thought. Yet I lingered in the crowd of strangers, comforted by their presence.

To my own surprise, I found myself wandering back to the gathering the next evening. I happened to look up at the pastor as he started to preach, and I began to listen—I thought he was talking directly to me. From the very back of the crowd of 250 people, I tried to sneak a look at Pastor Constantin just to see if he was looking right at me. I was relieved to see he wasn't looking anywhere close to where I was sitting.

He was preaching about the power of the Holy Spirit, how God could change lives even after the trauma of genocide. I lifted my gaze up to the pastor and then ventured to look around to see if anyone knew me. No one did. I was sitting there wondering, *How does this preacher, a stranger to me, know all my stories?* As he continued to preach, I started feeling joy. Something was changing in me. When he asked people to come confess their sin, I was the first to leave my seat. This was the day of my salvation.

It's hard to explain, but for a long time I didn't want salvation, though I knew all about it. God wanted me to have it, but I resisted. Before that night I was comfortable believing there wasn't a personal God who loved me. I knew if I chose to believe in God, I would have to face many questions that I didn't feel could ever be reconciled. I could not even fathom how to make sense of why evil prevailed in my country and God did nothing to stop it. *Why did Christian Hutus participate, and why did some of our clergy support crimes in the sanctuaries of the churches? If God was too weak to stop it, why would I call on him now?* Though I didn't have answers to these questions, the Spirit was prompting me to respond that night, and his will for me was stronger than my own brokenness.

I was still full of questions about God that night, but I recognized his voice speaking to me, the one I heard speak in the trees. I was humbled and wondered, *What kind of salvation did I receive? What would this mean?*

Wrestling with My New Identity

I went home overwhelmed by what had happened, keeping it to myself. The next night of prayer, I decided to stay home because I didn't want the pastor's words to make my heart so vulnerable again. Even the next night, I fought the urge to go back because I wasn't ready to hear more of God's goodness. But three days after I committed my life to Christ, I felt God speaking directly to my heart while I was sleeping. When I heard God's voice in my heart, it felt like rain and fresh wind blowing through me. It was like no other feeling I'd had before. God was still pursuing me, even in my slumber.

That night God spoke to me through a dream. I felt like I was moving toward something precious and beautiful. I was traveling ahead swiftly, sort of walking on air, leaving what was behind me as I moved toward this beautiful place. I didn't fully understand what it meant, but I knew the dream was from God, and my heart was expectant.

The next day I did go back to Restoration Church. The day was designated for prayer and fasting for all genocide survivors. I could tell these people praying were sincere and their prayers were powerful, so I decided to join them in their fasting. I hadn't prayed much before, but my heart for prayer kept growing in the following months, and I was beginning to grow as a Christian.

Initially I thought I had merely stumbled upon an unexpected gathering place in Restoration Church, but now I believe God guided my steps that night. He says that those who seek him will find him, and though I didn't know who God was on a personal level, I was searching for him, looking for truth. He met me right where I was. My church has restored me in ways I never thought possible—no longer am I known as *bapfuye bahagazi*, the "walking dead."

Dreams Grounded in Prayer

I remember vividly the call I felt in April of 1999 to pray and fast for my life's direction. I set apart a week to seek God. This was during the "Hundred Days of Mourning" that Rwandans observe each year with a series of memorial services. The loss that everyone was grieving over was hard to face, but God was present too, helping us through our pain. The room where we gathered at church was peaceful, which made me feel comfortable praying with other believers.

Three days into the fast, I went to my bedroom, turned on the radio, and heard a song from one of the memorial services. The Spirit told me to continue to listen to the music. The tears began to flow freely down my face as I remembered what the genocide had done, but as I wept I felt a freedom I had never known. I cried out to God on behalf of my brothers. I prayed for the widows and the orphans.

I turned off the radio. I sat still. I didn't pray using words, but God was talking to my heart. He said, "Your pain is going to be followed by joy." Though the tears kept flowing, joy was flooding my soul. It was the first time I had ever had that kind of joy. Years of silent suffering poured out of me.

God spoke to me, "Eric, you will never cry again as an orphan." During this time of prayer, he told me wonderful things, sharing with me his promises for my life—that I would have parents who would take me as their child and help me forget my pain. He was answering my prayers more quickly than I thought possible.

But I doubted one thing. I doubted that others in my life whom I loved could feel joy again too. How was God going to do that? I was thinking of my own hardened heart and knew how I resisted. How could he continue to change the ending of so many stories?

As I finished my week of prayer, my joy was constant. It was the beginning of my healing, and I started to pursue life with a new confidence that came from God, not my own abilities, though I so wanted to hold on to my pride. In January of 2000, many of the prayers said that week were answered.

More Open Doors

Shortly after this focused time of prayer, one of the local pastors in Rwamagana told me that Restoration Church of Kigali, our sister church, needed a chauffeur. So I went to the city to take a driving test. Everyone needed a job at this time, and this one paid well, so I knew I would be competing against other good drivers. About twelve people showed up for an interview. God gave me his confidence that day. That morning he led me to read Psalm 68:5–6: "A father to the fatherless, a defender of widows, is God in his holy dwelling. God sets the lonely in families, he leads forth the prisoners with singing." These verses were the promises I needed to hear. I did have a Father, and he was leading me.

As I entered the office before the test, I saw that some of the interviewers were my pastors, but they didn't know me well. I was the ninth one to be called in. As they asked questions, I felt as if I already had the job. I envisioned myself driving all kinds of people around the city of Kigali, sharing my story, making sure the car's chrome was always shiny. I told them about my experience as a mechanic and promised to take care of the church's cars like they were my own. I knew this was to be my new church home, where God would give

The cypress trees of Rwanda grow in dense clusters and can reach heights of over one hundred feet. (Photo by Kevin Diaz)

Eric's family knew the trees were not a well-known hiding place. (Photo by Kevin Diaz)

The Hillside Massacre was one of the bloodiest instances of genocide on record. The militia overtook the hills and murdered approximately 15,000 Tutsis.

Eric among the cypress trees.

During the writing of the book, Eric returned to the trees (now stumps) where he had hidden for fifteen days with his uncles. From left to right: Mugabo, Canisius, and Eric (Photo by Kevin Diaz)

Photo by Kevin Diaz

The militia dug a large hole on the grounds of this local school to bury the dead bodies, one of whom was Eric's grandfather. (Photo by Kevin Diaz)

Restoration Church in Kigali holds two thousand people. Pastor Bosco holds three services on Sunday—one in French, one in Kinyarwandan, and one in English.

(Photo by Kevin Diaz)

Eric works full time as a driver for the staff of Restoration Church. Most people in Rwanda do not have their own cars and therefore rely on drivers and public transportation.

Didine, one of the
orphans Eric cares for,
suffered a severe blow
to the back of her head.
She loves school and
enjoys studying.
(Photo by Kevin Diaz)

Photo by Kevin Diaz

The government
compound in
Rwamagana
was where thou-
sands of women
and children
fled for safety.
Egide found his
mother dead on
the steps with
baby Murindwa
still alive on her
back.

SHOUTS OF JOY
MINISTRIES
RWANDA
Isaiah 35:10

Eric with Fiston, one of the main interpreters for the book, along with some of the book team. From left to right: Egide, Tracey, Eric, and Fiston
(Photo by Kevin Diaz)

Mugabo Egide standing next to the isombe tree that protected him from a militia grenade.
(Photo by Kevin Diaz)

From left to right: Auntie Esperence, Eric, Mugabo Egide, and Murunzi Daniel
(Photo by Kevin Diaz)

Kigali Memorial
Grounds and Kigali
Hillside
(Photo by Kevin Diaz)

Kigali Memorial
Grounds
(Photo by Kevin Diaz)

Joyful Rwandan orphans (Photo by Joie Pirkey)

me family. The Lord was helping me give sound answers for each question.

"Eric, tell us a little about you," said one of the panel members.

"Well, I am an orphan of the genocide. I take care of my two brothers now. I am responsible and a hard worker. . . ."

I could tell the pastors were moved by my story of survival. I continued to share with them honestly why I needed this job. Finally the panel of interviewers asked me the question, "What Scripture helps you most?" I quoted 1 Corinthians 1:25–29:

> For the foolishness of God is wiser than man's wisdom, and the weakness of God is stronger than man's strength. Brothers, think of what you were when you were called. Not many of you were wise by human standards; not many were influential; not many were of noble birth. But God chose the foolish things of the world to shame the wise; God chose the weak things of the world to shame the strong. He chose the lowly things of this world and the despised things—and the things that are not—to nullify the things that are, so that no one may boast before him.

After I took the driving test and completed my interview, I was called back to meet with the pastors again.

"Eric, we want you to start working for Restoration Church tomorrow."

When I accepted, I felt like being a chauffeur for my church was a calling, not just a paycheck. Many times while I'm driving church visitors and pastors around, God speaks to my heart about how far he is going to take me beyond Kigali roads.

No Longer an Orphan

A father to the fatherless, a defender of widows, is God in his holy dwelling. God sets the lonely in families, he leads forth the prisoners with singing.

Psalm 68:5–6

When I joined Restoration Church in Kigali, I didn't know what I was going to learn from the staff of pastors. While I continued to serve as a driver for the church, Pastor Mukwiza, the senior pastor, began to invest in me, showing me love like I was his own son. I felt love from all the pastors I worked with, who always treated me like I was more than their driver.

Pastor Mukwiza told me that God had equipped me with all I needed to serve him in order to fulfill my life's purpose. Pastor was helping me to make sense of my past, my current work at the church, and my future.

"Eric, many people love you—children, young people, and the elderly."

"Pastor, why?"

"God is using your character to draw others to you. He has a plan for you to help heal the orphans of genocide. All your suffering will be used for his glory."

God had already been speaking these things to my heart, so I knew the Lord was confirming this through Pastor Mukwiza, whom I came to see as my spiritual father.

When victims of genocide suddenly find they are orphans, the assault on the heart is hard to describe. You instantly become a broken person. Survivors like me are a generation in need of love, wisdom, and counsel from older generations, though sometimes we don't have the ears to hear wisdom because of our issues of abandonment. Our self-image has been defined by what happened to us, and we need encouragement to better ourselves. Because I had to be a father to my brothers at such an early age, I didn't have time to grow up myself. Through my pastors, God was providing the guidance I needed. Though God gave me strength to nurture my brothers, I knew I needed to lean on wiser men and women to grow me into a godly man. He has given me back what I thought could never be given back to me—a loving family.

Pastor Bosco

Pastor Jean Bosco Habimana has also been a father to me. He joined Restoration Church about thirteen years ago. He and his family came back to Rwanda, their motherland, in

October 1995 after living as refugees for almost thirty years in the Democratic Republic of Congo. The government was pleading for all Rwandans to come back in an effort to encourage reconciliation. Everyone knew our only hope of survival was to become a unified people once again. Many Rwandese refugees who had been living for years in neighboring countries began returning. Pastor Bosco and his wife began to sense that God wanted them to come back and be part of the reconciliation process in our country.

After much prayer, they were convinced that God had work for them to do in Kigali. Pastor Bosco's family began attending and fellowshipping at Restoration Church and felt their own spiritual father was Pastor Joshua Masasu, the man who today has planted twenty-five churches in Rwanda. At the time, Pastor Bosco worked as an engineer and had his own company. I never tire of hearing his testimony, and I marvel at his heart for reconciliation:

> Though I had my own engineering enterprise, I gradually became more passionate to serve in our church programs than in my business. Because of this increase in passion to serve God, my wife and I decided to take another prayer retreat, asking God what he wanted us to do. . . . We both felt compelled to close our business, and straightaway, we returned our license to the government.
>
> Our conviction was confirmed when Pastor Mukwiza and others told us that God convinced them that we should serve as full-time ministers in this church. We closed our business in July 1998. We started our full-time ministry in Restoration Church in 1999.

Pastor Bosco has been an example to me—as a caring boss, an honorable husband, and a loving father. I know him as a man of integrity. He has helped me when I've encountered hard relational conflicts in ministry by exemplifying the biblical model to follow. Facing conflict is not easy for me because at the core of the genocide was senseless violence, division, and discord. To a genocide survivor, to have to face any kind of conflict feels like a sort of death sentence. We long for peace in Rwanda, and sometimes we live with a false peace because we do not face conflict properly. Our tendency is to ignore our relational struggles.

But my pastor has lived out what true peace should look like: you face your sin and the sins of others together as a family of God. Though I still fear any kind of confrontation, I have witnessed the fruit of this in my life. And I know it is making me a better leader.

I love to hear Pastor Bosco's heart for reconciliation. He is a mentor to me in understanding what forgiveness should look like in our churches and communities. God has given him wisdom that is fostering unity in our church as Hutus and Tutsis worship alongside one another, praying to the same God.

Reconciliation is a very costly thing to pursue in a country like Rwanda, where unbelievable atrocities toward humanity have taken place. To be asked to forgive those who murdered your family is an overwhelming request. To be able to take a step toward peacefully gathering Hutus and Tutsis together in church is nothing short of a miracle. Pastor Bosco knows the complex cultural issues and the fears that plague survivors. Yet he is not afraid to push toward the unity God wants for

us. He continues to foster a culture of forgiveness, support-
ing those who have made great strides. God knew I needed
this example in my life.

Pastor Bosco closely shepherded a gentleman in our church
named Karangwa Justin whose family was wiped out in the
genocide. While studying at university, he met a girl, Mu-
kangarambe Adeline, who was a member of our church.
Adeline's mother was in prison, waiting to be sentenced for
her active participation in the genocide. The two came from
different perspectives on the genocide: Justin, a grieving survivor; Adeline, a shamed daughter of a killer. Because of
God's grace and their commitment to reconciliation, they
moved past their hurts, were married, and had a child. Both
are active in Restoration Church and are a living testimony
to others who struggle with forgiveness.

Other young people have followed their example of reconciliation through the act of marriage. A Hutu gentleman
named Mbaraga Faustin and a Tutsi woman named Mu-
kashema Theresa came to Pastor Bosco to declare that they
too knew firsthand that reconciliation was possible and took
their vows of marriage as husband and wife. Such testimonies
transcend reason and speak to the power of God.

Our pastors still face the hard issues of a fractured people,
fifteen years after the massacre. But I'm so blessed that my
spiritual fathers have taught me to define our hope in the
bond of Christ; they want us to experience the blessing of
being a channel of restoration for others. Our church motto
is "Restored to restore." Our leadership believes we cannot
be true witnesses of Christ without living out a model of

reconciliation. And such a life is a sacrifice for any genocide survivor to consider.

Beyond being an example of living out reconciliation, Pastor Bosco has encouraged me to believe that I can be an overcomer, no matter what roadblock I may face. I remember a day when I was particularly discouraged about my lack of education; I wanted to master English and French but couldn't find the time. Pastor Bosco told me, "If people in the world who don't have the Holy Spirit in their life can make it, how much more able are you with God in your life?" His inspiration has enabled me to say with conviction that I can stand up and trust God for what I desire: a ministry in favor of orphans.

Parents from America

In 2005, visitors came to our church from America, accompanied by a Rwandese pastor by the name of Twagirayezu Darius. These Americans, Douglas and Joie Pirkey, spoke of their love for the Rwandese people, and I was deeply touched by their compassion. *Why should they care for us?* God was clearly speaking to me about these visitors: "These people are going to be a new family in your life." I had doubt in my heart that this could be possible. *Would God go to such trouble to send a couple from America to be my family here in Rwanda?*

I boldly asked Pastor Darius for an appointment to speak with him before he was scheduled to leave for the States. He agreed to meet me the next day, and I shared my testimony, explaining in detail what God was telling me about the visitors from Appleton, Wisconsin. Little did I know that God had already spoken to Joie and Douglas about me.

Before we met, Pastor Darius had told them I ministered to orphans. After hearing what I wanted to do to help the orphans of the genocide, Joie went back to her hotel to pray, and God convicted her heart to share her ministry resources with me.

The first day I met Douglas, we felt a connection that is hard to explain. As presumptuous as it sounds, he promised me that he would be guiding me as a loving father. I could hardly believe their generosity, but the Pirkeys asked me to come to their hometown and share my testimony with their community. They wanted me to share the dreams and hopes of the orphans of Rwanda, those whom our outreach, Humura Ministries, is trying to reach.

For three months Joie and Douglas showed me the love that was in their home. I was not treated as a guest or a foreign missionary but as a part of the family. I had to quickly learn culturally appropriate behavior in America, but everyone was patient with me and understood we had different customs in Rwanda.

I remember one night after dinner when Douglas asked me if I would like to help him clean up the dishes. I was taught that this is work for women. My first reaction was to feel insulted. He held on to my shoulders while we talked, and he showed me the affection I had received from some of my uncles back home. In Rwanda, we are very open with our affection for one another; though it's strange for Americans, you will see Rwandese men holding hands as they walk together. We sit on each other's laps and just talk, which is a sign of respect and admiration. So Douglas's physical affirmation made me feel like I was accepted. I knew Douglas was always honest with me, so I felt like I needed to listen to his advice and learn from him as a husband and father.

Joie and Douglas also gave me their perspective on struggles people have in America, such as how youth have wandered from God and how many struggle with depression. I love children, so I didn't understand why children pulled away from me when I would try to hug them or just say hello. Joie explained to me that children are taught to be afraid of strangers because adults try to take them away from their families to harm them. I wasn't aware of the problem of abuse and abductions in America—only of the abuse in Rwanda. Because I know what it is like to lose family, I pray for American children, just as I pray for the orphans in Rwanda.

My American family provided a safe place to process the genocide, away from my country. The distance was surprisingly healing, though I missed my home. When I'm with my family, I still feel I need to be the strong one. In America I could openly talk to Douglas and not worry about showing the pain that's still there. Douglas is very wise, and he helped me to see that it is not a sign of weakness to go through a grieving process.

When God promised to bring me parents, I assumed that this would be fulfilled within the borders of Rwanda. Yet he continues to fulfill this promise beyond anything I could have imagined.

Humura Ministries has been blessed by the generosity of Douglas and Joie through their ministry, Shouts of Joy, and their home church, Christ's Church of the Valley. I now feel like I have family all over the world.

In love he predestined us to be adopted as his sons through Jesus Christ, in accordance with his pleasure and will—to the praise of his glorious grace, which he has freely given us in the One he loves.

Ephesians 1:4–6

A Call to the Fatherless

Religion that God our Father accepts as pure and faultless is this: to look after orphans and widows in their distress.

James 1:27

Sometimes our church hosts pastors who come from overseas to encourage genocide survivors. One pastor I remember particularly well challenged everyone to find a place to serve God. I felt, again, that God was specifically speaking to my heart about serving him in ministry. The pastor preached on Joshua 1:5–9:

No one will be able to stand up against you all the days of your life. As I was with Moses, so I will be with you; I will never leave you nor forsake you.

Be strong and courageous, because you will lead these people to inherit the land I swore to their forefathers to give them. Be strong and very courageous. Be careful to obey all the law my servant Moses gave you; do not turn from it to the right or to the left, that you may be successful wherever you go. Do not let this Book of the Law depart from your mouth; meditate on it day and night, so that you may be careful to do everything written in it. Then you will be prosperous and successful. Have I not commanded you? Be strong and courageous. Do not be terrified; do not be discouraged, for the LORD your God will be with you wherever you go.

After his message, I kept thinking about the words "Be strong and courageous"—these were also the words my father shared with me before he passed away. Then I prayed honestly, "Lord, if you really are talking to me, how will this happen?" I was thinking how I really didn't have anything to offer God. I didn't know what I could possibly do for the Lord. I could barely help my brothers . . . I was homeless . . . I was still so young. But God kept these words of promise in my heart. And the faithful voices of all my spiritual parents continued to grow in my heart, giving me faith to step out.

On January 6, 2001, I was praying with my church at an overnight prayer meeting. As I prayed, my burden to help orphans was intense and heavy—I wasn't sure what God was asking of me.

I was crying out to God, "How can I serve you even more? How can I help orphans?" I pressed through in prayer, honestly sharing all my doubts with God and asking for courage. I knew he was calling me to a new level of trust in him before I could help the orphans. Because of the evil ideology that had divided Hutu and Tutsi for decades, I had to relearn how to trust again, and that included trusting God. I knew my relationship with God was stunted because I was withholding trust. My heart still questioned, *Where were you, God, when killers murdered my family?* Lovingly he continued to accept me and my questions.

Small Beginnings

I started to visit genocide orphans in their individual homes, which are not organized homes with guardians. Most orphans live in abandoned homes or makeshift shelters and have learned to exist without help of any kind. There were too many children for the government to support. I knew where to find most of them and prayed with them and talked with them. I continued to ask God, "What can I do?" God just said, "Start something!" So I went to my pastors to ask for their advice, and we prayed about all that was stirring in my heart.

With the blessing of my pastors, I took a step forward and gathered a number of orphans together. We had fellowship, prayed, and shared our genocide stories. I listened to each of them share their fears and what they faced in their own situations post-genocide.

"Eric, does God really love me?"

"Why should my life matter?"

"Will genocide happen again?"

I wanted to provide a safe place for them to ask the questions in their hearts. They began to trust me with their struggles. I decided to regularly visit them, house to house. The orphans I visited knew I understood what it was like to lose hope. In story after story, I heard the despair in their souls and their hunger for loving authority in their lives. Now it was clear. I finally knew exactly what to do for them. Even with no resources, I could be a mentor to them, sharing with them God's Word and what God had done for me. That was the gift God wanted me to give, despite my circumstances.

As I got to know the orphans better, I began to share openly my testimony and how I had escaped the genocide. Some were very comforted to hear it, and they were opening up to me too. Their hunger to hear God's promises was growing, and I took great joy in sharing many of them. The genocide had left few without physical disabilities. Many women were raped during the genocide, so the babies who resulted from this crime were often born with HIV. When I met such a victim, I tried to make them forget the infected white patches around their mouths and their swollen bellies, so they'd know they were beautiful too.

As I grew closer to the orphans and saw God's hand on them, I wanted to provide for them in more ways, like helping them with their schooling and their medical and nutritional needs. I knew some lived with families that were unkind to them, some even abusive, so I saw a need to build orphanages all over Rwanda that would give them loving house parents. New dreams kept growing in me.

While God had called me to begin this ministry for orphans in 2005, he also had been speaking to Joie Pirkey about Rwanda in 2004, all the way around the world in Appleton, Wisconsin.

Dreams Rising

That's the difficulty in these times: ideals, dreams, and cherished hopes rise within us, only to meet the horrible truth

128

and be shattered. It's really a wonder that I haven't dropped all my ideals because they seem so absurd and impossible to carry out. Yet, I keep them, because in spite of everything, I still believe.

Anne Frank

My weekend visits to the orphans were now something they expected. Of course, I wanted to be as consistent as I could and not break my promise to them that I would come every week. Trust had to be built for me to earn the right to share with them who Jesus is. On April 15, 2005, I planned a gathering and invited over two hundred orphans to come. Here they shared their own testimonies of survival. I could see the healing power of gathering together. I realized that we needed to meet quarterly. Each time we gathered, more came. The Lord ministered to me as I heard their honest confessions and struggles, which only made my compassion grow even more.

You could say Humura Ministries (*humura* means "restoration," or "take heart") began in my heart during that first gathering. The word "humura" is what a Rwandan might whisper in someone's ear who is deeply troubled and without hope. When someone says, "Humura, my dear friend," he is offering to share in the burden and comfort a broken heart. And this is what I believe God has called me to do. It is what Rwandans say when someone has a deep trouble and shares it with you and they are in tears and depressed and then you whisper, "*Humura.*" Now, it is an organized nonprofit ministry, and God continues to stretch me and challenge me to think bigger as he opens doors for ministry.

God had to help me see beyond what the orphans lacked so I could help them see God's dreams and hopes for their lives. What he showed me during our first meetings was that the orphans needed someone who cared and listened to them, first and foremost. I saw joy come to their hearts after they shared very heavy problems openly. The Spirit was healing them through the fellowship of other survivors. We were safe—together.

In reality I didn't have answers to their problems. They were too great for me to solve. I didn't have medical resources. I didn't have money to send them to school. But I could offer my prayers and give them a little of the extra money I earned as a chauffeur.

Though defeating obstacles had to be overcome, I had the support of my pastors and continued to seek out their counsel. My desire was to change the course of history through the orphans of Rwanda, to raise up the least likely ones, and I shared my conviction with them: they could be the generation to bring unity to our country.

"Eric, this passion you have is from God," asserted Pastor Mukwiza. "You are able to help these orphans because you have been an orphan yourself. They accept you because your life experience reflects theirs. They know they can be themselves with you."

Boasting in Weaknesses

The wisdom of Pastor Mukwiza helped me to see the deficits in my life, namely being an orphan genocide survivor, as a strength, because I could fully understand the struggles which gave me the ability to minister to others. This was a resource and a blessing I had not considered before.

It's been hard to see at times, but I'm beginning to grasp that God can do much more through my weaknesses than my strengths. In my country, poverty is considered to be from the hand of Satan, but I don't think that is completely true. When I offer up my lack, whether it is money, wisdom, or time, there is much more room for God to make up the difference. "Blessed are the poor in spirit, for theirs is the kingdom of heaven" (Matt. 5:3).

Most orphans have so much to overcome. Some are street children, and others live in homes where they are not wanted. Their medical needs range from serious malnutrition to fatal diseases. They need to speak with counselors to heal their trauma. The more fortunate orphans have some type of sponsorship to pay for their education. Not all orphans are able to attend school. But all of them have dreams.

Without God in their lives, the youth of our country will try to fill their pain with other substitutes—like drugs, crime, or prostitution. Some have convinced themselves that they are the source of life's problems and shouldn't have been born. No one has taught them that they have been created in God's image to do great things, that life really does have purpose and meaning.

Humura Ministries continues to grow, and one day I want to minister in this capacity full-time. Each year God gives us more resources than the year before.

This year we had almost two thousand orphans come to hear the gospel during our conferences. Not all the orphans invited actually come. I contact them through our church and many of the orphans I know have cell phones. I try to use the limited media we have available, which is through ham radio. This wouldn't have been possible without Joie and Douglas's commitment to the orphans of Rwanda and sharing the resources of their ministry, Shouts of Joy Ministries. Their financial support is humbling, but even more humbling was the love shown through the missions team from their home church, which offered to come and volunteer. Because of the continued support that comes all the way from America, the orphans feel loved in special ways; they see God's people coming together, which lets them know that the world really does care.

Humura Ministries is starting to receive calls from other areas of the country where we have not been. Continually we see God expanding our vision as he meets our needs. No matter how poor they are, most orphans have access to a cell phone, giving us greater access to them. I am always encouraged to get a call from one who needs to share their worries with me. Knowing these broken children are speaking out and not keeping their feelings inside keeps me going and hoping for more opportunities to help. Currently our goal is to meet the objectives God has laid on our hearts, with his help:

- teach and proclaim the good news of Jesus Christ
- live a life of charity according to John 15:12, "Love one another, as I have loved you" (KJV)
- write resources to show the works of God in the lives of people

- provide educational needs (tuition, uniforms, and supplies) for primary, secondary, and university studies as well as for vocational schools
- help the vulnerable youth of Rwanda such as genocide orphans, AIDS victims, and street children
- participate in the fight against HIV/AIDS by organizing prevention programs and educating youth to receive testing before marriage

All Christians are called to come to the aid of orphans and widows, according to James 1:27. I want to be faithful to God's call to the fatherless, despite the setbacks the ministry faces, and to never give up on a child.

Hope for Rwanda

Then I saw a new heaven and a new earth, for the first heaven and the first earth had passed away, and there was no longer any sea. I saw the Holy City, the new Jerusalem, coming down out of heaven from God.

Revelation 21:1–2

Hope is alive in Rwanda. People want to join in what God is doing. Our country is being restored through those responding to God's call. From Congo to America, servants of God are feeling a burden to just come. And in this chapter I want to share just a couple examples of the good things happening in Rwanda.

Pastor Joshua's Ministry

Pastor Joshua Masasu, who started Restoration Church in Rwamagana, was the first pastor I met after the genocide ended. He brought hope back into my life. His ministry is impacting thousands in Rwanda because of his obedience to God. Listen to his story:

I was in Kinshasa in the Democratic Republic of Congo serving as a pastor there for Jerusalem Ministry, which was a ministry to reach Rwandan people, many being refugees from previous genocides. God clearly spoke to me in July of '94 after the official end of the perverse war: *"Go to Rwanda now and bring the message of the cross, because it is the only hope after such destruction."* I didn't want to go. It was very hard for me to leave my family and go to a broken country without any tangible support—except I did have my faith in God.

When I reached Kigali, God spoke to me about Ezekiel and the valley of dry bones. He reminded me how this prophet spoke over the scattered dry bones and a vast army was raised up. God was clearly showing me he wanted to do the same for Rwanda, that he was going to raise up a restored people who once had very dry, broken hearts. He asked me to start a family church and to name it Evangelical Restoration Church. The church was to be known as a place where everyone could find a parent, brother, sister in Christ. Our first Sunday was on October 9, 1994; then our official launch followed on October 16 in Kimisagara Youth Hall.

Because I didn't live in Rwanda when genocide happened, I have had to rely on God to help me through problems I haven't experienced myself. Sometimes the situations genocide survivors share with me are very complex and the right answer seems gray. Most of the time, when my wisdom is just not enough, the Holy Spirit intervenes for me.

I remember one woman coming to my office, begging to know God's will. She was a victim of rape and was expecting a child. She wondered if God wanted her to mother this child, a child who would be a reminder of her attacker. As her shepherd, I knew her situation—no money, no husband. I sat and listened . . . and prayed for the Spirit to give me counsel. As we prayed, the Holy Spirit specifically showed her she was to keep the baby and God was going to raise up this child in ministry. I shouted, "Hallelujah!" I knew God had to impart wisdom only he knew.

The very difficult question that people share with me continually is, "Where was God when I was almost killed and crushed by hate?" Spiritually I was challenged with how I could be a witness to God's love, though I didn't go through such a trial.

Pastor Joshua is a man of great hope, full of miraculous God-stories, and when you are around him you feel like you can take on any obstacle. He loves people, and he loves God most of all. Sensitive to those stricken with poverty, he has struggled with seeing church members without food, money, and shelter. But over and over, God has provided a miracle for a widow or a family in ways Pastor Joshua couldn't. By the grace of God, Pastor Joshua has planted twenty-five parishes under the arm of Restoration Church throughout Rwanda.

Hope from America: Shouts of Joy Ministries

When I went to America, I heard about how God was giving many people a burden for the country of Rwanda. Africa is a vast continent, and my small country is about the size of the state of Maryland. Yet somehow God is stirring hearts to come to this easily overlooked country.

My spiritual family from America, Joie and Douglas Pirkey, have committed to join God in the work he is doing in Rwanda. When I first met Joie, she shared with me a specific vision God gave her in June of 2004:

> There were hundreds of hills. Moving. There were all of these little motions about the surface. I looked more closely and could see that they were tiny black heads. I did not recognize the landscape, so I asked God, "Where is this?" The Holy Spirit answered, "Rwanda."
>
> "Why are you showing me Rwanda?"
>
> "Feed my people."
>
> "I can't feed this many people."
>
> "Feed them with your gifts. Your joy, your ability to trust, your education, your love for Douglas . . ."
>
> As he spoke this, I was panicking about not wanting to go. . . . I began to ask God how any of this was going to happen. As crazy as it sounds, God clearly spoke, "A man from Africa will come prophesying about a revival in the youth for Wisconsin. He will facilitate you going." That's really all I knew of the puzzle and I had to be patient and wait.

About a year later, Bernard Blessing from Ghana came to Appleton, Wisconsin, to preach near Fox Valley, where Joie lived. She had heard Bernard was from Africa, so she asked to have fifteen minutes with him. Just days before, Pastor Darius had called Bernard, asking him to look for a person from Wisconsin to join their team of ministers in Rwanda; God was setting up a meeting.

Joie explained to me, "After I met with Bernard, I asked the Lord why he was sending me to Rwanda. He said, 'I want you to bring Rwanda the ability to trust, which you have here in the Fox Valley area, and I want Rwanda to bring America the freedom they have to worship me freely and joyfully.' I did ask God to explain about the importance of trust for these people, as I knew nothing about genocide or their cultural issues at the time. He explained that trust is what undergirds a country's economy and supports a social structure."

With a whirlwind of doors opening through relationships, God miraculously provided for Joie and Douglas, and in 2005 they made their first trip to seek out ministry opportunities in Rwanda.

On their first trip to Rwanda, Joie and Douglas met Pastor Mukwiza as they were trying to discern what God wanted to accomplish in this trip. He was very kind to them. The first time they entered the church building, the Lord impressed upon Joie that he was going to raise up one staff person who worked for Pastor Mukwiza. She believed God was saying, "This won't be an obvious choice, but a man will be raised up and used to spread the word of forgiveness and reconciliation internationally."

A few days later, Darius took Douglas and Joie to Rwamagana to meet me. We gathered in a hotel conference room, where we met over fifty of the orphans under the care of Humura Ministries. As Joie was confronted with their dismal circumstances, she prayed to the Lord, "How in the world am I supposed to help these kids? Their needs are so great, and my resources are so limited." God told her to be faithful with what she had, like the boy who gave his lunch to Jesus to feed the multitudes.

A young orphan girl stood up and confronted Joie, saying, "Many come asking for our stories, and they take our pictures, saying they are going back to America to raise money for us. But the money has never come. We do not have enough food. . . . There are so many things we do not have. You say the Holy Spirit told you to help us, so what are you going to do for us?" The orphans, most of them in their late teens, clapped as she sat down. Joie was left feeling even more helpless.

But she sat thinking again about the loaves and fishes, convicted that with the small offering of just one boy's lunch, Jesus fed five thousand. So she prayed for God to show her just one orphan she was to help. I was the one. Gathering up all the courage she had, Joie spoke to the orphans' concerns. "I have no resources to give you, but somehow I have been sent to help you. I also need you to ask the Lord what he wants you to do to help Rwanda. He asks all of us to give whatever little bit we can, and through that offering he can feed thousands."

I was shocked when the orphans stood up and clapped. She had somehow earned their trust and penetrated their cynical hearts. They were outcasts with only a trail of empty promises behind them. I knew God was leading us all together.

Hope without Limits

Unplanned and strategic relationships continue to form in my life. God is bringing a diverse people from all faith traditions, ethnicities, and various occupations to come and join God's work here. A new optimism blows into the city streets of Kigali and surrounding villages. God is clearly speaking to people about Rwanda and about our people. Efforts of reconciliation are happening through the church and our government. My church has been one contribution in efforts to bring Rwanda back together as united Rwandese people.

Every seven years Pastor Joshua and his leadership team discern God's vision for all twenty-five parishes of Restoration Church. From 1994 to 2001 our churches focused on evangelizing and gathering people from different backgrounds to create an atmosphere of "family."

From 2002 to 2008 we focused on healing, deliverance, comfort, and restoration. Pastor Joshua wanted survivors to relearn that every soul is valuable to Jesus. In October 2008 our leadership reflected on all the ways God accomplished this goal, and we celebrated together. Throughout the twenty-five parishes, we have seen God bring about miraculous healings and bring liberation to many. Some of the most moving stories of reconciliation have taken place.

I'm excited for the next seven years. The focus will shift toward strong biblical teaching, preparing people for discipleship and missionary efforts. Genocide can quickly mar a person's perception of God. We are ready to learn more about how big God really is and study more intently what Scripture says about the Father, Son, and Holy Spirit. We will be more willing to take up our crosses.

We see our pain differently now; we know we don't have to fear it, but rather we are empowered to enter it with full knowledge that God is present. Our pastors were wise to know in the first seven years of ministry that the hearts of genocide survivors were bound up. We couldn't move on to a greater openness to God without a safe, loving spiritual family to surround us. Now God's Word can properly take root in our hearts because our community and our leadership have given us the medicine we need. We don't have to live as bleeding people; we can be healed. Many survivors will eventually be strong witnesses to the restorative power of Christ. We get stronger every day.

The sacrifices being made to help restore us are astounding, and miracles happen daily. Everywhere I turn as I drive through the streets of Kigali, I hear laughter and sense a new anticipation in the air. Small businesses are sprouting up. Churches are growing. God-ordained marriages are forming, giving Rwandan children secure homes. We're alive again.

PART 4
A People of Hope

The Healing Flame

But suddenly, Nebuchadnezzar jumped up in amazement and exclaimed to his advisers, "Didn't we tie up three men and throw them into the furnace?"

"Yes, Your Majesty, we certainly did," they replied.

"Look!" Nebuchadnezzar shouted. "I see four men, unbound, walking around in the fire unharmed! And the fourth looks like a god!"

Daniel 3:24–25 NLT

For Rwandans, April brings the hope of rebirth, but not without a cost. We long for spring, but the shadows of winter linger because we are reminded of our enemy. Remembering brings a downpour of tears, and a chill settles in our bones. Shelter and a warm bed do not bring the comfort of restful sleep. We know when we approach the wintry-spring season, old wounds that have not healed are waiting to be reopened. We know we have to face it—the healing is yet to come.

Entering into the Pain

I have suffered through many night terrors. I've relived the horrifying chase of the devils close to my heels. Some nights I've dreamed of my own death. Other dreams bring the lifeless faces of my family before my eyes, covered in decay. I've been shaken out of such terrors to the smell of fresh blood in my room.

It's estimated that 90 percent of all genocide survivors are still experiencing trauma at some level. Though Rwandans have vibrant, wide smiles, there is deep, unresolved pain in the hearts of survivors. Some have been forced to change jobs because of unresolved trauma, such as an elementary school teacher who stopped teaching because he could not stand seeing his students who were the same age as his children who died. Many survivors have developed unusual habits induced by post-genocide stress, called *ihahamuka* (trauma, literally meaning "breathless with fear"). It can manifest as antisocial behaviors in young people or promiscuity in young girls or widows. Sometimes a survivor acts out through excessive drinking, showing strong aggression and irritability which can be directed toward anybody.

The "Hundred Days of Mourning" begins the first week of April and continues through to July. Our government, nonprofit organizations, and churches all assist survivors in the grieving process, hosting hundreds of memorial services and candlelight vigils throughout the hundred days. These services are a safe place for families to come to heal. Healing cannot come any other way; we have to face the horrors that are unresolved in our hearts. As thousands gather in churches and at various memorial sites, we are reminded that none of us is alone.

April 7, 1995, began the first organized period of mourning. At the time I was still living in severe emotional pain, and I had to avoid the ceremonies in order to remain stable. All the evils I had endured were still fresh in my mind. Though I didn't let my family know this, my heart was still bleeding and the pain was too great for me to be able to formally participate.

Many survivors are still too traumatized to remember. Many of us still can't talk openly about genocide, even with our family members. But each memorial service provides an opportunity for designated families to remember their loved ones with honor. Corpses are still being found in holes dug by the Interahamwe all around Rwanda. Family members are notified when the body of a loved one is found so they can prepare to find the strength to pay their respects and give their loved one a proper burial provided by the government.

Honoring the Dead

In 1996 I went to one of these memorial services. I remember the experience vividly. I had received notice before the event that the bodies of my family members had been identified. I could recognize the physical features of many of the bodies because they were still in the early stages of decomposition, though I did not expect this. I recognized some of my family by their clothing, as their faces had turned to bones. The orange and purple fabric of Auntie Verena's *mishanana* (dress) reminded me of her vibrant faith. As I lowered each of my loved ones down into a more honorable grave, I realized their dignity was living on through my brothers and me.

Grandmother, my father's mother . . . my aunties, Musanabera Verena, Mutegwamaso Drocelle, Mwenzikazi Vestine . . . my dear cousins, Gikudiro and Dukunde. I took a moment to remember how much I missed them.

For the first time since the genocide, I allowed myself to recall the beauty of my mother, Mediatrice. I closed my eyes and saw her dancing to a native song. She moved with poise even when she wasn't dancing. I saw her brown arms waving above her head as she danced, and I remembered how her hugs comforted me so many times as a boy. She was known for giving love away freely. She cared for so many, even after she was left a widow from my father's illness. That part of her lives on, as she taught me and my brothers how to care for others too. I was at peace knowing the militia could not take her from inside my soul.

I remembered Grandmother's gentle eyes as I mourned in public for the first time. And I remembered my dear aunties who always welcomed me into their homes like their own son. They all had died around this particular grave site. I was dizzy and weak as I said good-bye, but I had to do it so my family could mourn properly. I wanted to run but knew this was my responsibility. I felt like I was the surviving father of my family and I could help give rest and relief. This realization was a turn toward my healing.

The physical act of burying them had a profound impact on me. I felt intense pain, but I also felt a healing flame enter into my heart. When the period of commemoration was put in place, I just thought it would be a time to bury our loved ones. I didn't know God would use this time to begin my own healing process.

Rwamagana Memorial Service 2008

During this year's Hundred Days, my American family, the Pirkeys, along with their missions team, were in Rwanda. They wanted to attend the Rwamagana memorial service with me and my family, though this was a very daring act of love on their part which I didn't expect. There was no way I could fully prepare them for it. But I knew part of their reason for coming was to help Rwandans mourn and to weep for those who could not weep. As they shared the burden of genocide with us, I felt some of the darkness lifting. God was helping me to move on but not forget.

As we all entered the government building, the service began with prayer offered by a local priest. He read the liturgy, and we sang about the love of God. Looking around, I estimated there to be close to a thousand in attendance. We sat in front of an elderly couple dressed in traditional Rwandan clothing. I looked around to see who would be called upon to bury their family members. You can tell these Tutsis apart by the purple neckerchiefs they wear to indicate their role in the service. The young boy acolytes came down the aisles robed for the ceremony. I watched them light the candles all around the platform. The service felt stiff at first. I could tell the mourners were still self-conscious, unsure when to hold in their emotion or break down.

Those who experience *ihahamuka* and cannot release their pain live with a poison that deteriorates their bodies and souls. The ones who cry out are cleansed; they are delivered from the loneliness of silence.

After the homily was given by the bishop, we made our way outside to the mass grave site. It is customary to bring a picture of the deceased and give a brief eulogy over the grave site. I began to pray, "God, help me move away from the consequences of genocide so I can help others." God answered this quickly. For the first time, I allowed my heart to hear the testimonies of other families in a way where I felt their pain too. The healing flame that had started in me earlier was melting away more of my hurts. This was the first time I was able to truly mourn in community with others. God was clearly speaking to me that he is calling me to weep corporately with my country—Tutsi and Hutu alike—and that he wants the whole world to weep with us too.

I could tell my American friends were struggling to stay, as some wondered if their presence was offensive to the mourning survivors.

Mugabo served as a pallbearer for the service and was getting ready to walk toward the mass grave, but then he turned to Douglas.

"Douglas, would you come with me down to my family's grave?"

Fighting back the tears, Douglas graciously declined. He felt it was an honor he should reject out of respect. Mugabo understood and took his place at the grave.

As the burial segment started, a woman behind us began to have a flashback. "Jeanette, Jeanette . . . run!" she yelled, screaming over and over the name of her daughter. Violently trembling, she fell backward into the crowd and collapsed to the floor. She had injured herself, and an ambulance finally arrived to carry her away from the service. Something as simple as an arm gesture can trigger this type of manifestation of trauma. Therefore the dynamics of such memorial services can be unpredictable, and counselors and medical workers are available to assist the mourners.

Hutus were there too, to remember. No tribe escaped the ill effects of genocide. Hutus have to face the shame daily, whether they were actually perpetrators or not.

I saw Rwandans watching my American friends weep. Some looked shocked. Some confused. I believe those silently grieving were drinking in the empathy of Americans. They saw that the world does have compassion for them—that others care about their pain. God is using our collective pain to knit us together again as a country. "Blessed are those who mourn, for they will be comforted" (Matt. 5:4).

A Future Memorial Site

Memorial services grow in number each year, and mass grave sites continue to be erected. No terrain or region of Rwanda escaped the massacres. During the genocide our rivers and lakes were overflowing with blood. Thousands and thousands died in our lakes, trying to swim away from their hunters. Others were thrown into rivers, which carried bodies to the borders of neighboring countries. Some were shot with bullets and fell victim to the flow of the blackened-bloody waters. There is a river, River Kagera, that flows between Tanzania and Rwanda, and a large thunderous waterfall flows from it. People come from all over to see the majestic waters. During the genocide its beauty was stolen as bloated bodies fell over into Tanzania every few minutes.

My desire is to set up memorial services all around our shores and on our riverbanks. I want to take back the rivers and lakes the genocide stole and allow God to make them places of healing. Occasionally I will see a few families gather at Muhazi Lake during the Hundred Days to pray and bring flowers. For a long time after the genocide, I didn't want to look at Muhazi Lake, the battleground where Mugabo endured unimaginable violence. The lake reminded me of the blood of Tutsis, so I tried to act like it didn't exist anymore. But I realize now that it is really God's lake; the devil only tarnished its beauty for a time. Now I like to think of the waters carrying the blood of Christ, which has freed me and my brothers from sin. I know Jesus won't forget one drop of blood that was innocently shed.

I want genocide survivors to swim and play in our beautiful rivers again. I want the marsh and the lakes to be healing pools for those with deep scars. I want to see churches baptize people in God's love at these rivers. And Rwandans will come out of the waters a resurrected people. But we first have to look back and remember.

Remembering is something God asks us to do over and over in the Bible: "Remember the Sabbath day by keeping it holy" (Exod. 20:8). "Remember your Creator" (Eccles. 12:1). The Israelites were experts at remembering, building altars of thanks and celebrating festivals to be mindful of God's mighty acts of provision. They had much to celebrate: the parting of the Red Sea, the supply of manna in the desert, the cloud by day and the pillar of fire by night. In remembering, they knew God was faithful, and it fortified their faith for the next battle ahead.

All of us who are Christians are asked to remember too. The violence of the cross is in front of us each time we take communion—"Do this in remembrance of me" (Luke 22:19). Though it isn't easy to face, we are asked to remember the blood he spilled out for us. When I embrace his suffering for me, it gives meaning to my own. I know it also forces me to re-member the pain of others. And God doesn't want me to forget the innocent blood that was shed over the hills of Rwanda. The act of remembering holds something very sacred—it makes us more grateful. We have to be willing to remember our pain so we can comfort and offer a place of healing for others.

In my mind's eye, I see rivers that flow with freedom again, clean and alive with froth. I see crowds with bright candles emitting the light of God—candles floating on the water to bring a healing flame as they remember. People come to weep together and celebrate the miracles of God since the genocide. I am praying for God to show me how to establish such future memorial gatherings. I believe he wants us to come to the shores with forgiveness in our hearts. I feel like Moses—the violence-stained waters did not overtake me! "By faith the people passed through the Red Sea" (Heb. 11:29).

Seventy Times Seven

Then Peter came to Jesus and asked, "Lord, how many times shall I forgive my brother when he sins against me? Up to seven times?"

Jesus answered, "I tell you, not seven times, but seventy-seven times."

Matthew 18:21–22

I want the world to know that genocide in Rwanda did not happen by accident. It was calculated. Executed by radicals. Rooted in sin. In the history of humanity, nothing so devil-inspired just casually happens, as we have learned. In 1994 the conditions of my country were such that this horror could occur once again.

When Hitler slaughtered six million Jews during World War II, the world said, "Never again." And yet genocide continues to happen around the world and is still a reality for the continent of Africa. And we ask, "Why is this?" I believe part of the answer lies in the heart. You cannot look at the complexities of the hell that is genocide without looking at the reality of evil and how it can corrupt a heart. The heart is where we store up hate, prejudice, jealousy, and unforgiveness. In order to understand, we must admit what sin can do.

Before I became a Christian, I did not feel obligated at all to forgive the killers. My reconfigured mental state after the genocide was blinding me. I viewed the world very differently after my heart was raped of believing in the goodness of man. God had to heal my distorted view. Humanity had let me down, and I didn't know how to forgive. To me, it was dishonoring to the dead to forgive the Hutu extremists.

Naturally I thought, *The killers who vengefully took the life of my family—they aren't seeking me out, asking for my forgiveness. Why should I, the victim, be the one to offer pardon?* But even if they had sought me out, I didn't know how to forgive. I didn't know about the freedom that forgiveness offers.

History teaches us how to respond, and sometimes it teaches us to not respond, to not forgive. My family were victims of Hutu radicals in all three genocides, and I had not witnessed repentance from them firsthand. The third genocide, the one I survived, proved that the Hutus still held on to their hatred and therefore, I was justified to hold on to mine. So without knowing how God can change a heart, I was resigned to accept that Hutus would never change—that hatred was an irreversible generational curse. It seemed to be in their blood to kill, like a reactive, sinister ritual.

As I talked with my grandfather when I was a boy, he was always honest with me about the reality that genocide could happen again. But this was a hard concept for me, since I played with Hutu children. Rwandan culture values big-heartedness. My father was a very kind and generous man. I remember Hutus and Tutsis alike would come and seek his advice, and he would seek theirs out equally as well. No matter what tribe you were from, if my father liked you, he would give your family whatever they needed. But there was always that seething, festering wound of our past—one of your neighbors could quickly turn and choose to run with the devil. This made me build up a wall in my heart of unforgiveness, suspicion, and wariness. These are the demons I have to confront though the shadows of my hunters are long gone.

Loving Your Neighbor Again

I remember my first encounter with a Hutu after genocide. I was walking down the street, and I felt overcome with anger and panic. My breath stopped as we passed by one another. I was particularly fearful whenever I would have to pass by more than one Hutu walking together.

I tried to come up with a rational view of humanity. Perhaps God created mankind in two types—those who are good and those who are bad. I knew instinctively such a conclusion was too simplistic. But at that point in my life I was not able to see that God also created Hutus in his image. But then I would hear of Hutus who rescued Tutsis during the genocide, so I was left with unresolved theories. *Some can show mercy? Some risked their own life for Tutsis?* More and more evidence said that not every Hutu supported the genocide.

The segregation among Rwandese was obvious when people started returning to their villages. Our country was in a relational crisis. You could see the bitterness on the faces of Tutsis and the shame in the eyes of Hutus. Tutsis were struggling to just survive a day, as their possessions had been plundered. Hutus were trying to figure out how to approach coexisting with Tutsis. Such difficulties seemed irreconcilable, so we lived separate lives. Eventually we would have to face each other.

Throughout the long months following the genocide, I found myself trying to get a stronger grip on all the memories I had of my cousins, great-aunts, sisters, and other family members. The thought of forgetting anyone who was killed made my mind sick. I would try to remember them, to honor them, all by name: Mutegwamaso Drocelle . . . Muvubyi Emmanuel . . . Nyiramajigija Verediane . . . Kanakuze Mediatrice . . . Umutesi Shushu . . . Muhongayire. . . . I would not allow myself to forget even one, no matter how distant a relative they were. Bitterness felt like my right as a survivor. I savored its flavor, and though I thought it was nourishing my broken heart, it was a kind of poison that God had to expel.

When I heard my pastor share the gospel, the battle in me started. I knew God was asking the unthinkable. If I wanted God to forgive me of my sin, I would have to forgive the enemy.

After I had been attending Restoration Church for a time, I would leave feeling so encouraged by the speakers who came to minister to us. They spoke often of how God could heal and mend our brokenness and of the deep love of God. I desperately needed to know of God's love. Hearing countless messages about the need to forgive others was hard to swallow. I knew it was God speaking, but I did not want to confront this truth. When the apostle John ate God's Word in Revelation, some of it tasted bitter and even gave him stomach pains (see Rev. 10:10). Much like this, as a new believer, I was learning quickly that God's Word comforts but also disciplines.

The various servants of God who came to speak to us knew our country's history; they knew we were in need of restored hearts. God would often lay on their hearts the medicinal words we needed, which was most often a word about true forgiveness. Initially, when a visiting pastor from a foreign country came to preach on forgiveness, it would sting twice as much, though I knew it was true. Such sermons were not easily accepted by genocide survivors. Understandably, we felt entitled to not trust, to not offer forgiveness. History was on our side in our suspicions.

But God began to show me that he was beginning to heal my heart. He was showing me that healing had to happen in me before I could even attempt to forgive. As I opened more of myself to God, I experienced more healing. And soon he began to point me toward the walls I had set up in my heart. He showed me they were a false security, walls created by genocide. I was beginning to believe I didn't have to live this way and I really could be free.

For a time it seemed I could feel a healing happening deep within me. I tried to fiercely trust God and surrendered to him all the hate I had tried to hide in my heart. God's plan for my life was about more than my job, my ministry, or any title I would pursue—it was about making me whole. Everything God was asking me to do, I felt a freedom to obey him and do, as a child of God, not a victim. More and more I wanted to fulfill his will, not my own—even when it meant going beyond the restricting walls I had built within.

As I became more involved at church, I found myself in common circles with a Hutu named Comrade Uwamungu. We met through our youth fellowship at church. I was not naturally inclined to seek out a Hutu's companionship, but I also knew that true peace would not come until I learned to be open and welcome the relationships God was placing in front of me. I was fighting with the Spirit, who was telling me that my true family was found within the body of Christ. I had been comfortable with just loving God and not necessarily those God wanted me to love. Slowly I began to see that God was doing something unexplainable in me. I wanted to be Comrade's friend.

As we grew closer, Comrade and I talked about what had happened to our country. He openly showed his grief for me as he intently listened to me share the circumstances that I had to overcome as a victim. When I saw his deep concern toward me, our friendship grew. The Holy Spirit continued to speak to me about him, telling me to seek his friendship. Still I continued to argue in my heart with God. I kept reminding God that even Hutu Christians were killers during the genocide. How could he expect me to pursue a relationship with someone who might kill me?

But then I heard God speak to me in a way that silenced my rebuttals. God said, "Eric, I did speak to the Christian

Hutus during the genocide, but they did not listen to me. That is why Christians acted the same as those who did not know me. If you do not listen to me, you are just like the Christian Hutus of the genocide."

That day I accepted and obeyed the Holy Spirit concerning my view of Hutus. When I opened my heart to both Hutus and Tutsis—to Comrade—God began sending people to me just to say, "Eric, I love you as a brother in Christ." Such affirmation was enabling me to also open my heart to love, which had not been possible before. Comrade is one of my closest friends today, and we still pray together. What had once seemed impossible to me continues to happen again and again in my church. I'm in a place in my life where healthy relationships are growing. The tribal lines are becoming blurry, and we are moving toward God's plan of being known as just Rwandans—God's people.

I remember too the first time I was confronted with the life of Joseph, described in the book of Genesis. This was one of the first stories God used to illustrate to me what true forgiveness looks like. As I pondered the life of this remarkable leader, I realized that the promises God gave Joseph were fulfilled only after he went through severe trials. His own brothers tried to kill him and sold him as a slave because of their jealousy and hate toward the favored brother. Through much persecution, Joseph knew that all things would work out for the glory of God. The trials he would have to endure were no rival for his faith in God's sovereign plan. Without the privilege of suffering in his life, he would not have known the beauty of forgiveness:

When Joseph's brothers saw that their father was dead, they said, "What if Joseph holds a grudge against us and pays us back for all the wrongs we did to him?" So they sent word to Joseph, saying, "Your father left these instructions before he died: 'This is what you are to say to Joseph: I ask you to forgive your brothers the sins and the wrongs they committed in treating you so badly.' Now please forgive the sins of the servants of the God of your father." When their message came to him, Joseph wept.

His brothers then came and threw themselves down before him. "We are your slaves," they said.

Genesis 50:15–18

If you personally have been profoundly hurt by another person, it's tempting to want to hold on to the anger and the pain. Maybe you, like me, have been hurt by someone you thought was safe. Perhaps you are afraid to offer trust to one reaching out to you. I believe relational pain is the slowest kind to heal. A price must be paid to hold on to bitterness; a price must be paid when we open our hearts to forgiving others. God wants so much more for the brokenhearted than for us to be paralyzed by sorrow and hurt. He wants us to lean hard into him, past the pain. Just as he did for me, he will lead you beyond your suffering as he begins to show the blessing that is beyond the struggle.

But Joseph said to them, "Don't be afraid. Am I in the place of God? You intended to harm me, but God intended it for good to accomplish what is now being done, the saving of many lives."

Genesis 50:19–20

Have you ever thought of your trials and your enemies as a path toward God's will for your life? When we move our eyes off the enemy, we can see the other side of our pain and allow God to make us new people. Forgiveness takes prayer and time. Relationships are messy because we are all sinners. Who is God asking you to forgive? Even before Jesus took his last breath on the cross, he asked his heavenly Father to "forgive them; for they know not what they do" (Luke 23:34 KJV).

I want you to know of my struggle so that you too may feel the call to forgive. Bitterness can rob you of all God has for you. I believe my life was spared in part to offer a message of forgiveness to others. Perhaps you have turned your heart away from God because of unexplainable hurt without realizing it, as I once did. You may have shouted out in anger at God, *Where were you when I needed your protection? Where were you when you could have easily stopped the enemy from harming me?* I am here to tell you that he hears your cries for mercy, though you may feel like they fall on deaf ears. He sees your pain. He sovereignly sees. And he is much bigger than our passing feelings that we think give us control.

Because of our humanness, often we feel we cannot forgive unless we fully understand. But often God asks us to let go of our need to know the unexplainable and simply trust. The reality I face every day is that genocide is an unexplainable evil—one of the most complex strategies of hate the enemy has ever invented. As the days pass, God continues to give me a better understanding of my own fallenness and my desperate need for his mercy. No earthly justice I can come up with would look like God's love, and that is something I trust beyond my finite mind.

Forgive Even When It Doesn't Make Sense

Experts agree that the 1994 Rwandan genocide was rooted in racial intolerance, just like the Jewish Holocaust. The government allowed messages of hate in the media, and discrimination was openly practiced. In both atrocities, political uncertainty destroyed the trust between communities of people. When this happens it is much easier to manipulate a group of people to commit grave acts of sin. Both races—Tutsi and Jews—were being eradicated by an ideology that labeled some to be subhuman.

Though we can study such conditions in a country, much still remains unsolved by sociology. Some evil acts the world has known cannot be explained with theories, but rather we have to reflect on the condition of each human heart without God. Without God, we have the potential to become monsters, even killers. Jesus says if you hate, you are a murderer in your heart (see Matt. 5:21–22). All of humanity is in need of the forgiveness of God, and no one is beyond the reach of God's long arm.

When I decided to become a Christian, I knew the Bible taught that our salvation comes at a price—it means forgiving "seventy times seven" (see Matt. 18:22 NLT). This is my cross to bear.

I feel now a different kind of dilemma. The genocide left me with faceless enemies. I can't look the Interahamwe in the eyes and seek reconciliation, as many fled or are in prison. It is easier to be mad at an abstract group of deranged radicals than it is to confront a killer face to face. This was a real strategy of the radical Hutus. They killed in groups so no one had to face this responsibility as an individual. They also hid, seeing themselves as faceless killers not individually guilty of genocide. So I too have hid behind hating a mass of killers, not wanting to be confronted with the real face of an individual Hutu. Still I pray God will show me fully what forgiveness looks like.

Perhaps one day I may meet one of the killers face-to-face. But mostly they still remain faceless enemies that I witnessed in masses below while I was hiding in the tree. I desire to love the faceless Hutus I have not met who tried to kill Mugabo, who killed my mother, who killed my sisters. I must see them as individual people in need of God's grace. Slowly, God is helping me to see them as real people who are in need of his forgiveness too. They too bear the image of God. Mother Teresa once said, "Hitler was also an image bearer of God." I'm learning that God's capacity to love unconditionally is above my understanding of love and forgiveness. I know I'm not there yet.

God isn't asking me to dismiss my pain and just blindly trust and move on. He is just asking me to let go of my false crutches of security and let him protect my heart. For this part of my story reminds me of the growth I still have ahead of me, where I feel most vulnerable. God continues to challenge me to trust and to forgive. I am confident that he will continue to teach me about the mysteries of forgiveness, the most difficult lesson for a genocide survivor. To my surprise, I'm finding that forgiveness is one of the greatest gifts a victim can offer. Any survivor knows that complete reconciliation can't come without forgiveness, and for that we have to appeal to the supernatural strength of God.

The Privilege of Suffering

There is no pit so deep that He is not deeper still.

Corrie ten Boom

Life's sufferings can be the very things that keep us from believing God is really there. But they also can be the very things that draw us to him. Sufferings serve as a powerful source of discipline in our lives. I'm not sure I would have recognized my need for God unless all was stripped away from me. Perhaps I would be living too attached to my family's wealth, relying on other worldly things for security—fleeting things. Perhaps I would have never opened my heart to the orphans of my country. I even venture to think the genocide was my salvation from self. I don't mean to say that God was the author of the genocide—I do not believe that. Only the devil and his fallen angels, with the cooperation of a deceived people who have rejected God, could execute such a plan. But

I believe God uses the evils allowed in this world to draw us to him. The paradox is clearly there.

How could a good God allow suffering? It was a question that never left me after the genocide, and worldly ideologies left me with no real answers. I started seeking God's truth. I wanted to know the history of God's people in the Bible. I wanted to learn about Christians who had suffered and persevered. As I became more acquainted with the stories in the Bible, I realized that among all the people of God, none escaped suffering. The righteous and the unrighteous alike faced suffering. I was stunned to learn that this theme was consistent from Genesis to Revelation. It was strange to my thinking that God used pain as the very foundation of a testimony. Throughout history, suffering has been what has cultivated the growth and faith of his people. Noah. Abraham. Joseph. Moses. Elijah. Job. The apostle Paul. Not once did God ignore the pain of his people. I was beginning to understand that God was profoundly near during my sufferings, even before I knew him personally.

I felt a connection with Daniel, who was thrown in the lions' den. His enemies wanted him to die a violent death with no possible way of escape. But God miraculously shut the jaws of his predators. The Lord preserved my life, even though I was not a man of prayer like Daniel. However, my prayers that were not full of faith were still heard. He answered, despite my unbelief.

James 1:2 instructs us to "consider it pure joy" when we "face trials of many kinds." Suffering is never wasted in our lives, from God's perspective. His ways are often counterintuitive. Our sufferings are valued by him, and he wants us to use them to fortify and strengthen others who are in need of hope (see 2 Cor. 1:3–5). The history of the world proves we cannot remove suffering from this life, no matter how many times a society strives to improve the quality of life through medical advancements, technology, or our standard of living. We cannot create a utopia, no matter what man-made ideologies we try to follow.

Rwandese people all have different views of suffering. Some participated in the genocide. Others were victims. And some Rwandans were not in the country at the time of the killings for various reasons. I know survivors who lost their limbs and some who were victims of rape. Some would still say they have been forsaken by God. Those who carried out the crimes of genocide face another kind of suffering. They walk with disgrace as they know they have lost trust among their countrymen. They exist as outcasts. No one in my country has escaped the sufferings of genocide.

But I'm learning pain is universal. The problem of pain and disappointment is not exclusive to my country's atrocities. Every person's life has a measure of pain that can be used in destructive ways or in dignified ways.

When I think of America I think of a blessed nation with promise, opportunity, and wealth. America is the land of the free. Yet I also know many live in bondage, whether it is spiritually, physically, or financially. You may be reading my account of the genocide and think that your suffering is not important to God compared to mine. Or maybe you feel that mine is nothing compared to your heavy burdens.

I believe that God is compassionate toward all who suffer, no matter the magnitude. Perhaps you are facing the devastation of divorce and you cannot imagine how God will rebuild your life. Or, you may be angry at God and struggling with why he did not protect you as a child from abuse. Pain can come from living with private shame for something you did. God spared my life so I might have a chance to tell you, *all things are possible with God*. Maybe you have endured a trial that seems to continue on with no sign of being resolved, and you don't see a solution and don't have the strength to pray for a miracle. I am here to say, *all things are possible with God*. Though the darkness can feel like it will overtake you, remember the work God does in the night seasons of life.

> Then Moses stretched out his hand over the sea, and all that night the LORD drove the sea back with a strong east wind and turned it into dry land.
>
> Exodus 14:21

Rwandese people are still hurting, trying to work together, trying to remember, trying to forget. As I look around at genocide survivors, I want them to know that we have fellowship with Christ in our sufferings. Douglas says, "God will make a ministry out of your misery, and he will give purpose to your pain."

Mugabo struggled, like me, with how a loving and merciful God could allow the genocide. But as he began to hear God's Word, he was drawn to the gospel because of Jesus's suffering; he was also a man rejected by his people.

Mugabo's Conversion

Mugabo began to go to church with me on Sundays a few years after my conversion and was beginning to understand more about God as Father. One Sunday, a blind man came to preach.

"There is a reason why I am blind," claimed the preacher. "There is a reason I was born like this. Maybe you are here and have been through something that has deeply hurt you—but there is a reason for it."

Mugabo hadn't heard someone speak of suffering in this way before, and I could tell Mugabo's heart was softening. The preacher went on and shared the story of Jesus healing the blind man:

> As he went along, he saw a man blind from birth. His disciples asked him, "Rabbi, who sinned, this man or his parents, that he was born blind?"
>
> "Neither this man nor his parents sinned," said Jesus, "but this happened so that the work of God might be displayed in his life."
>
> John 9:1–3

Mugabo intently listened, and then the Spirit whispered: *There is a purpose to be found in your suffering.* He then allowed his mind to wonder why God wanted him to survive. He allowed his heart to say, "Perhaps God does want to be my Father." He went forward and asked Jesus Christ into his life.

Mugabo now shares his story with other orphans:

171

At sixteen years old, I decided I could trust God. Life looked a lot different after that Sunday I heard about the blind man in the Bible. I knew God was the only one who could use my suffering to help others.

When you are a child and have scarcely escaped the clutches of death over and over, it is hard to make sense of it. Now as an adult, I see God much more clearly. That doesn't mean I can explain why God allowed genocide to happen again in my country. I cannot know why a hostile Hutu chose to murder one child but not me. I don't know why the road I chose to take led me to the safety of the RPF. I don't know why God thought it wise for Eric, me, and Murinzi to survive but not my mother.

I take great comfort in knowing I serve a God who is in control; that evil can never overcome good no matter how bleak life can be. God is firmly and unquestionably in control. He is infinite; I am finite. And in his infinite wisdom, the way God allowed my mother to escape the ills of genocide was to find ultimate healing in heaven. For me and my brothers, God found it wise to not yet take us from our earthly home, perhaps in part so we might tell our story of God's grace and providence.

When I reflect on the unleashed evil that plundered the hills of Rwanda in light of God's sovereignty, the ghosts of genocide no longer dominate me.

I don't completely know how God will use the suffering in my life, but I do know it has given me a compassion for the orphans that I would not have otherwise. The poverty the orphans face is indescribable. You can see the disowned street children gather in the district sector, creating their own families, just trying to pursue a peaceful life though they have nothing.

Because I once was an orphan and now God has taken me as his son, I too can be a father to orphans and point them to my heavenly Father. When you survive something as heinous as genocide, when you've actually smelled the scent of death, yet come back to life, an unshakable faith is formed at the core of who you are.

Mugabo made a decision to change his sorrow to joy, to let Jesus take away his sin. Right after the genocide he was always angry and mad. But when Jesus came into his life the gnashing of teeth was replaced with God's love. Mugabo used to spend many days overcome with sadness. Now I watch him and marvel—he can spend the whole day laughing.

Grace Found in Suffering

I believe that Job is a Christ-figure of the Old Testament. He experienced every kind of suffering life can bring—financial hardship, sickness, lost relationships. Job even cursed the day he was born (see Job 3:1). But in the end he had the same response as Christ Jesus: "Lord, your will be done, not mine." God's rebuke was not because Job had questions about his suffering; rather it was because he forgot his place, which was under God's authority. He forgot to respect God's sovereignty.

As God is growing me in understanding the mystery of suffering, he continues to use it to show me hidden treasures in my life. I've learned lessons through my trials that I could not have learned any other way. I know God can provide when you have nothing to give. Graciously he has helped me learn to love my enemies, even when I want to run from them.

Most people would say that persevering through a problem made them a better person, but one must make a conscious choice to see it as an opportunity to grow instead of allowing a bitter root to take over. You have to want to see the blessing of it. Job 38:1 says, "Then the LORD answered Job out of the storm." God did not wait until after the storm was over to speak. In the midst of it he answered. I wonder if just the blessing of his presence is something we are to learn through the trials. If he is present with us, then grace is present. I've missed living with that truth, as sometimes I just focus on the difficult circumstance I'm facing. But I know if I take my eyes off myself and seek him, I'll find him there in the midst of my storm.

Storm of Grace

Lyrics by Tracey Lawrence
Music by Dee Rohrbaugh and Kevin Diaz

Trees bowed to the ground
Dust whirls
Deafened by wind
Still I listen for you
Thunder and lightning
Driving rain
Who is the author of this pain?

Dark shadows surround
I hide
Hoping to see
Through this cloud of my pride
Cold and trembling

Shades of gray
Out of this darkness I see your face

Let it rain, let it rain,
Let it blow 'til I believe
Let it fall, let it fall,
Until I see your beauty
In this storm of grace

So I'm going to ride these waves
I'm going to dance in the wind
Because your grace
Is calling me into this storm

Rivers still rage
I pray
Future's unknown
Yet I follow your way
Healing waters
Mystery
A storm of grace has covered me

Let it rain, let it rain,
Let it blow 'til I believe
Let it fall, let it fall,
Until I see your beauty
In this storm of grace

Trees bowed to the ground,
dust whirls . . .

Orphans of Faith

For the accuser of our brothers, who accuses them before our
God day and night, has been hurled down. They overcame him
by the blood of the Lamb and by the word of their testimony.

Revelation 12:10–11

Genocide left 120,000 Rwandan children without parents.
Rwanda has one of the largest orphan populations of any
country. Thousands and thousands of homes still remain
parentless today.

When Americans come and meet genocide orphans, our
visitors are surprised that though they are poor, the children
don't beg for money. They mostly want to know what you
think: *What should I do with my life? Do I have good character? Does God love me?* They are starved for godly wisdom.

Loving them has contributed to my own healing. Perhaps I'm
drawn to caring for them because I know they are defenseless,
like I was in the tree. I know they will not turn on me as my Hutu
neighbors did. This young generation is resilient and strong.
They want the world to hear what God has done for them.

The Gospels are full of testimonies of God's power from eye-witnesses who saw Jesus heal the sick and raise the dead. When the blind man received sight, he went and told others. When the Samaritan woman received living water from Jesus, she went back to tell what happened to her, and "many of the Samaritans from that town believed in him because of the woman's testimony" (John 4:39). Revelation 12:11 says we overcome the evil one by the word of our testimony. When the orphans *tell*, they experience God's power at work in them; when others *hear*, their faith is strengthened. When we gather to share our stories, I know the devil runs out the door when the smallest, weakest orphan stands up to attest to the goodness of God.

A Boy Called Ndacyayisenga Emmanuel

The very first orphan I reached out to was Ndacyayisenga Emmanuel. I tried to care for him as a father. He survived the genocide along with his four sisters. Both of Emmanuel's parents were killed alongside my mother. After the militia had shot his parents, the children were all found alive in a group. The militia didn't try to kill them but just left them to starve. This was not an act of mercy; the killers knew that dying of starvation was a more torturous, slow death.

Just as the bullet went through my mother and hit my baby brother, the same was true for Emmanuel's mother and baby sister. The baby survived the bullet wound.

Through the brutal days of genocide, groups of militia would approach them, asking Emmanuel, "Why should we let you and your sisters live?" They were barely hanging on and couldn't respond, too weak to communicate in an intelligible way. So the militia mocked them and sent them to stay with a man who was known as a crazy hermit in their village.

"This crazy man is not smart enough to care for them. May they suffer under his roof," reveled the proud Hutu. I don't know if the militia ever went back to mock them, but this crazy man did care for them, and they were provided for until the RPF came to rescue them. Miraculously, all five survived.

Emmanuel had an even more difficult road ahead of him than I did, having been left with the responsibility of caring for four children—at age twelve. But today Emmanuel shares his struggles openly with others and attests to the power of God in his life.

An Orphan Called Innocent

Innocent was eight years old when the genocide happened. He witnessed the murder of both his parents, watching in agony along with his siblings. Innocent is the only surviving member of his family. Often he shares his testimony at our Humura Ministries conferences. Whenever he speaks, I see the orphans become stilled by the miracles surrounding his story. He speaks with profound conviction that God is working through every moment of life, emphasizing the healing power of God. Intently he looks in the eyes of orphans and calmly says, "We are all safe in God's hands now."

Suicide was very common among both Hutu and Tutsi Rwandans after the genocide—some wanting to escape the pain of shame and guilt for participating, and others unable to cope with surviving. Before Innocent became a Christian, he tried to commit suicide three times due to his severe trauma. At just eight years old he made his first attempt. Left alone as an orphan, despair grabbed his heart, so he found a rope, made a noose, and tied it to a tree. He jumped out of the tree, but the rope broke, releasing his neck. His failed attempt left him angry, thinking, *How can I try again tomorrow?*

The next day Innocent confessed to a friend that he wanted to end his life. This friend told him to put oil in his ears, convincing him he would die right away. He poured the oil in both ears but woke up the next morning to find he was dreaming of death but was still alive. "Why did this not kill me?" Emmanuel shouted.

He continued on, determined to find the best way to end his life. He asked another man, who said, "If you take water with a syringe, then put it in your muscle, it will not take long for you to die." Innocent was determined to make this third attempt work. He pressed the needle into his arm and waited. Nothing happened. He was still alive and breathing.

This was when he turned to God and committed his life to Christ. He was convinced God had thwarted his plans. Today Innocent loves life and continues to inspire orphans to persevere, no matter how hard it is to hope for something better.

A Girl Called Didine

Didine is a shy, reserved sixteen-year-old. She is not one who will approach you, but she allows you to come to her. Sometimes it can be hard to know if a personality is shaped from trauma or if it is simply an orphan's character. But Didine endured much suffering as a toddler. She too was caught in the crossfire of bullets which were meant for her mother—one striking the back of her head, another penetrating her pelvis. The physical pain she has requires skilled medical attention that Rwanda cannot yet provide for her.

During the genocide, Didine was almost a year old. Her mother was carrying her on her back—both were shot. After the shootings of the week, the militia would come on Friday to dig holes for the dead bodies, but Didine and her mother were still alive when they were thrown into the hole.

A despised man from the village saw the young baby was really alive and said, "Don't take that child; give me the baby. I will take care of her." This man was very poor and was a recluse. The Interahamwe laughed at his intentions and figured the baby would die, whether in the hole or in the man's pitiable house. Though considered inept and a lowlife, he took care of Didine. He fed her goat's milk, which Rwandese do not normally consume. He nursed her wounds and provided nourishment, and after a week's time he learned from others in the village that her aunt was nearby, so he took Didine there.

Today her aunt cares for her, along with four other orphan relatives who survived. They live in the east province of Rwamagana with many needs unmet, but all the children have the privilege of attending school. Sometimes they don't have enough money to pay all the school fees, so they often have to miss semesters and then repeat classes.

Didine is a beautiful, wide-eyed girl with a calm poise about her. She will tell you her favorite color is red, and she loves to study French. You can plainly see the gash in her neck which has caused a permanent tilt in her neck. The internal damage in the area of her pelvis has also caused her health complications. She quietly carries around the aftermath of the genocide.

Didine doesn't openly share her thoughts about the men who maimed her. But I'm certain she has drawn her own conclusions, as you can feel the sorrow she carries around with her even as she plays games with other orphans at gatherings. I'm curious what she might become in the future; she is very bright, and I know God has a plan for her gifted mind.

When we are together, I try to lighten her spirit and make her laugh so she might be more open with me. I've been surprised to learn how optimistic she really is about her future.

A Girl Called Uwimana Jaque

Jaque was seventeen years old and from a wealthy family, which made them a target. The Interahamwe came into her home and took hold of her father. Her mother and two sisters were forced to watch the cruel acts of torture leading up to his death.

The killers made her father hold a mattress over his head and then asked him to set it on fire. As the flames flared, his hands, his arms, and the top of his head were instantly set on fire. Jaque's father threw the mattress away from himself. He said, "I have no conflicts with any of you, yet you only choose to attack me because I am Tutsi." With severe burns, Jaque's father was moved to a roadblock and forced to lie in the road naked. The cruel hunters then sliced his torso in half with a machete, which disemboweled him in front of his family, who watched his torturous death.

Jaque, her mother, and her sisters were then taken to the Catholic church in Kigali. There her sisters were raped. Both sisters lost their minds completely. As a witness to the horrible crime, Jaque experienced trauma that left her bedridden for months, which caused her legs and feet to swell because she could not get up. A friend decided she needed to see a voo-doo healer in town, but on the way she insisted to be taken to the God of Christians. A pastor prayed for her, and she was instantly healed.

Jaque is still homeless but is currently enrolled in a trade school.

A Girl with Many Names

Young girls were brutally raped throughout the days of geno-cide. When the militia came to kill a family, they often spared the lives of young girls so they could have their way with them. Most often a girl was passed around to the whole group of killers, so the killers could gloat in their perverted control.

Victims of this crime are afraid to speak out. Their shame runs deep at knowing they were only spared to be used over and over again. Please pray for these silent victims.

Testimonies to Come

I see such extraordinary testimonies growing around me every day. God has richly blessed Rwandans in the midst of poverty, though our country is considered to be a fourth or fifth world country. Hope and faith are strong in these young hearts.

Many genocide survivors have overcome much more than I have and won't have an opportunity to tell America their stories. The beauty of God is that he uses our differences, our similar struggles, and our life stories to unite us. Perhaps God used Joie and Douglas Pirkey's story to encourage you to step out in faith and be a missionary to orphans in Rwanda. Maybe Mugabo's story encouraged you to have faith like a child, or maybe Innocent's resilience helped you to be thankful for another day of life. I don't know what words of hope you need to hear, but I know there is hope for everyone. God loves you and has a special plan for your life. His signature work can be seen in all of us. I can't wait to hear the testimonies of those I've yet to meet.

Rwanda Today

So we're not giving up. How could we! Even though on the outside it often looks like things are falling apart on us, on the inside, where God is making new life, not a day goes by without his unfolding grace. These hard times are small potatoes compared to the coming good times, the lavish celebration prepared for us. There's far more here than meets the eye. The things we see now are here today, gone tomorrow. But the things we can't see now will last forever.

2 Corinthians 4:16–18 Message

The doors are opening for Rwandans to take their lives back. I believe God is raising us up to give back to others so that the world can see a kind of hope the world has not known. We are coming together as Rwandese, though our history suggests it is impossible. The government continues to support genocide survivors in reconciliation efforts. Gacaca (which means "justice in the grass") has been one of the admirable efforts to heal victims. Rwandan courts convene where the crime took place and Tutsis have an opportunity to hear truth from the perpetrators and work toward reconciliation. The gacaca courts push toward justice and have been a big part of healing our country.

People in America are praying regularly for our orphans. Shouts of Joy Ministries continues to support us in sacrificial ways. Restoration Church congregations here in Rwanda continue to share their support with Humura Ministries. And more orphans are accepting Christ into their lives and dreaming big dreams. I praise God for what he is doing right now.

Conferences of Hope

Because of Pastor Joshua's faithfulness to answer God's call to build churches of restoration, I have opportunities I would not have otherwise. What if he had ignored God's call to leave the Congo; would there be twenty-five Restoration Churches today? I'm humbled to think of my church's support of Humura Ministries and of the orphan conferences we had in 2008. We hosted 1800 orphans and widows and gave them seats of honor at Restoration Church. With a team of loving people God put together, we were able to provide a lunch for every orphan, transportation, and a fun program where they could share laughter and hear God's Word.

Our church choir sang, then my brother Mugabo gave his testimony, sharing his story of survival with the orphans and widows. Then a group of orphans performed a dance to a song about surviving and forgiving. Their feet kept the beat of freedom alive in the sanctuary. As I looked around, I was humbled by how God sent so many people to share in serving the conference, how many spiritual fathers I had, and the new friends God had brought into my life, even from as far as America. A Shouts of Joy missions team came to help us this year. Pastor Tim Snell from Appleton, Wisconsin, came to share his message, "Hope on the Road to Emmaus":

I want to talk about "Finding Hope on the Emmaus Road." I want to paint a picture of the setting of our story this morning. Two men are on the road; one is named Cleopas and the other is nameless. They are returning from a traumatic weekend. From Scripture we know they were believers in Jesus. They had been to Jerusalem to celebrate Passover, hoping to see Jesus.

Unfortunately they learned that Jesus had been handed over by the religious leaders and had been crucified. And so here they are on the road home, discussing the events that have transpired. All of us here today have an Emmaus Road. The road may represent your entire life. The road is a picture of our relationship with God. No matter what your road looks like, in the end, what matters is how we view God and relate to him on the way to where we are going.

When we are on the journey, we will encounter discouragement. Imagine learning that the one you thought could save you was crucified. All hope was lost for these two men walking away from Jerusalem. We all know the pain of discouragement. Sometimes our heads are downcast and we forget to look up and see. . . .

As the men on the road talked and discussed these things with each other, Jesus himself came up and walked along with them, but they were kept from recognizing him. He asked them, "What are you discussing together as you walk along?" Their faces were downcast.

When we are at our greatest level of discouragement, it is difficult to recognize that God is really with us. . . .

When we are discouraged, it is easy to want to quit. To turn our backs on God. But sometimes the dreams God crushes along the way are so we can dream bigger ones. . . . Finding hope on the Emmaus Road is all about finding God. You see, it isn't our circumstances that offer us hope; it is the living Jesus who is right beside us if we open our eyes.

After Pastor Tim's message, you could feel hope floating all around. The orphans more readily smiled; they were sitting taller.

The different speakers during our conferences all gave a testimony of hope. Temo Augustine, a man who was born blind, is one of six children, and the other five were killed in the first and second genocides. Temo survived all three genocides and today is married with children. He joyfully shouted, "If God can take me, one who has been blind since birth yet without sight escaped the trails of my hunters, you too, orphans and widows, have hope!"

God brought orphans and widows to our 2008 conferences from all over the surrounding areas of Rwamagana and Kigali. The ministry was able to pay the taxi and bus fees so they could come. We also provided quality counseling for the orphans, which was a remarkable benefit because very few quality counselors are available to survivors with trauma. My pastors brought hope. My American friends brought hope. And the orphans also brought hope.

As I spoke to the team from Shouts of Joy Ministries, I could also see how the orphans had touched them. When you see so many eyes searching for a way to fill the void in their hearts, it can be hard to face them. With a crowd of a thousand, you can avoid looking into their eyes, where you can see their pain. But I saw all the American team members kneel and look into their eyes and give them individual touches. Asking their name. Learning their favorite color. Giving hugs. Courageously loving. God was asking all of us to share in the orphans' pain. But even though their suffering is still there, mixed with joy, what you remember is their dignity.

Seven Years of Prayer: From 2009 to 2016

While I was on a plane to America, God gave me a new hope. I believe God is calling us to a concert of prayer for seven years to specifically pray for the healing of orphans. I want to organize conferences and gather all the youth of Rwanda, not just orphans. I believe God will use this time to bring all the youth, no matter if they are homeless or have good families, to come together and worship Christ. I believe miracles will happen.

In his book *The Purpose-Driven Life*, Rick Warren strikes a chord that resonates with every human heart: we all want to live with purpose. But the cynical worldview of today has caused many young people to wonder, *Why am I here? Does life even matter? Is there a God?*

I believe Rwanda, a once dead country, may be the nation God uses to show the world life does have purpose, it isn't a meaningless random act of the universe, and none of us are alive by accident. The evidence that we are becoming a resurrected people is coming forth now. Hutus and Tutsis are celebrating weddings together again. Joy is seen in the midst of suffering. People are turning to God for healing. Life is becoming beautiful again.

But I think God is going to take us to an even deeper level of love for one another than my country has ever known. I believe that Christ, being the great reconciler, is going to knit us together as a nation with his bond of peace. He wants to obliterate the philosophies of hate we have known. He will give us a greater love for each other that will require a greater sacrifice. Our identity will come from him, not our tribal name. If we can overcome, anyone in the world can. I long for the day when all Rwandans have a message of hope.

I know this is a universal problem—the youth of our world are losing hope. I dream of bringing youth from other countries to gather in Rwanda, to see and experience the beauty of Africa in a country that has been renewed by the grace of God. I want American kids who have lost their parents to divorce, drugs, or death to find hope in a generation who once had no hope in sight. I want the world to see Rwandese youth worship God.

I think when we bring about a love for the diversity of God's people, a new kind of healing will come to the world and to his church.

As I drive around the city streets of Kigali, chauffeuring God's beautiful people, I dream of bigger roads I will travel, roads where he leads me to minister messages of hope and forgiveness to those in need. I know he will show me how to get there.

Africans, Asians, Caucasians from the Americas and Europe coming together to shout out hope for the world; thousands reflecting the image of God over the hills of Rwanda; young generations in a unified voice saying, "Genocide will never happen again"—I'm praying and dreaming of such a holy day.

> Because of this decision we don't evaluate people by what they have or how they look. We looked at the Messiah that way once and got it all wrong, as you know. We certainly don't look at him that way anymore. Now we look inside, and what we see is that anyone united with the Messiah gets a fresh start, is created new. The old life is gone; a new life burgeons! Look at it! All this comes from the God who settled the relationship between us and him, and then called us to settle our relationships with each other. God put the world square with himself through the Messiah, giving the world a fresh start by offering forgiveness of sins. God has given us the task of telling everyone what he is doing. We're Christ's representatives. God uses us to persuade men and women to drop their differences and enter into God's work of making things right between them. We're speaking for Christ himself now: Become friends with God; he's already a friend with you.
>
> 2 Corinthians 5:16–19 Message

My Return to the Trees

Recently I returned for the first time since the genocide to where the faithful cluster of trees used to stand. My three surviving uncles have gathered there together for years to remember. It's a safe place—a memorial site for them. Only the stumps of the trees remain, but my uncles have marked the spot as sacred and continue to visit often. It's their place, where much healing has happened for them. For them, it's as safe as home. I found myself surprisingly comfortable there. I never thought I'd return.

"I see the holiness of trees. I have a respect for them. They extended me grace when humanity turned into rabid dogs," said Uncle Innocent as we all gathered.

Uncle Canisius added, "When genocide ended, I looked up at the trees wondering where the rest of the world was when it all happened. Did they know Rwanda even existed? Why didn't anyone come to save us while we were being persecuted? After a time, I was able to look up at the trees, move beyond the whys, and be grateful that people are starting to come from all over to remember, to acknowledge what happened here. Before genocide, I used trees to build houses and fires. But they have more value to me now; I see them as created by God. They can save a life."

My wise uncle Nyombayire Jean Marie Vianney told us all, "When I look at any tree, I see the image of God. But their beauty was hidden from the enemy as we watched the killers massacre thousands below us. It was like the trees were whispering to us, 'Stay here, we will be your refuge, we know God.'"

A short distance from where the grove of cypress once was is a prison. Many of those who carried out the genocide are now incarcerated there. You can now hear the singing of Hutu prisoners. The radical Hutus' hateful chants are now songs of heaven, grace, and forgiveness. Some are now Christians and have repented for their crimes. I was once a prisoner in the trees; they are now prisoners just a ways up on the hill. That day with my uncles I lifted my gaze and saw the fruit of God's work all around me. The wild sounds of hate have been silenced.

My uncles explained to me that some of the inmates came a while back and chopped down the trees for their own firewood and means of survival. So the very trees that nourished us and kept us safe were cut down to nourish those who were once our enemies. "I laugh now and consider the trees to be a symbol of reconciliation," said Uncle Canisius.

I began to try to reconcile all I heard from my uncles. The Hutu radicals who were sentenced to prison on the hill in front of me, the very men and women who were caught for their crime of wiping out over a million people in one hundred days, are surviving where we once survived. Only God could bring our stories together in such a merciful way.

I wanted to remember this new outpouring of grace I felt, what it felt like to return to my battleground in good and healing ways. I sat on each stump, laughing as I scurried to the next. I felt a joyful freedom in returning. One more time I lifted my head toward the prison. The Rwandan breeze gently refreshed me, and the grassy hills looked like how I might imagine the hills of heaven. I was to be grateful for the prison on the hill. I marveled at the grace that had come to my life despite the genocide, and realized that the very same grace of God had found the hearts of my enemy. Perhaps that is one reason why God tells us to pray for our enemies— because he knows that a changed heart can turn an enemy into a friend.

193

Conclusion

I am grateful that I've shared with you my story of suffering, which has allowed me also to share my hope. You are not alone in your sufferings, whatever they may be—there is fellowship when we share our burdens.

I now embrace my suffering and even accept genocide as a part of the legacy I will leave behind to the world. God has used my loss and pain to foster hope in my life. But such an assertion doesn't really make sense without God. My prayer is that my testimony will lead you to seek help from God, to find out how he wants to use your trials to bring hope to others. We often don't see what God is preparing for us in the midst of trials and what he invests in us through hardships. But I know now through the pain that he is mightily at work.

I did not see him clearly when I was hiding in the trees. He was a distant idea, a God I had heard about but did not embrace. I could not see his hand on me, just the branches holding me up. But now I am free, and I look up at the trees of Rwanda and think how much more real God is to me than even the trees before my eyes. I am a changed life! He is my reality. I am grateful for the trees that gave me a safe shelter. I respect God's wisdom in where he has chosen to grow a bush, fill a river, or plant the roots of a tree. And now I can even trust him to determine when he offers life and when he takes it away.

All he creates is with purpose and beauty. There are no flippant, random acts in all of creation, because God is a God of order. You were created for a purpose and made in his image, to live where you live and know the people you know. Acts 17:26–27 says, "From one man he made every nation of men, that they should inhabit the whole earth; and he determined the times set for them and the exact places where they should live. God did this so that men would seek him and perhaps reach out for him and find him, though he is not far from each one of us." Maybe you are trying to make sense of unexpected failures or a series of devastating hardships. I challenge you to place them in God's hands. I know he will be faithful to show you the way out, and he will take your life to a much more beautiful place than you can find on your own.

I do not worship creation, nor the trees. I live to worship my Creator, my Father, the One who made them. The enemy wanted to destroy me, and he wants to destroy you. He wants us to live paralyzed by our trials. He seeks to kill and destroy humanity because he knows we were created in the image of God. Sometimes the pain seems so unbearable that we try to numb it in destructive ways—suicide, consumption, and hating others.

Remember, our struggles in this life are temporal. They do pass. Look beyond the pain and see the joy that awaits you.

Brothers and sisters in Christ, I pray that you will patiently endure your trials, for you do not know what God is planning for you after they have passed. You just might change the world. I am alive to tell you God is real and he saved my life. My prayer for you is that you use your life to serve others. Be a catalyst of hope and be amazed at what God does with what you offer to him. Look up and see your Father, maker of the trees.

Epilogue

by Tracey Lawrence

It was 6:00 a.m. on the dot, and daylight was just creeping in. I woke up my first morning in Rwanda to the most unexpected, angelic sound: "Hallelujah, our God reigns, hallelujah . . ." From my bed I fell into the trance of this sweet, African melody that echoed through the surrounding amphitheater of hills—just one voice singing freely, with no care of who might hear. This first light's song gave me faith and courage to enter into the individual testimonies of genocide I would hear in the days to come.

Incongruously, my first impression of Rwanda was one of joy and praise, not the pain and sorrow of civil war. I lay there in the quiet discerning that a great hope was in store for this country. This country, the "land of a thousand hills," which had been an open grave for over one million corpses, was echoing the praises of almighty God.

I had the privilege of meeting Eric Irivuzumugabe's family, who are all heroic genocide survivors. All were very eager to tell me their stories of survival, except those still too traumatized. But even such family members wanted to be present during the interviews to support the efforts of this book so the truth is known. I found them to be brave, friendly people who generously shared smiles with strangers. Their eyes showed me the depth of their souls and communicated more than I could gather through an interpreter. To be in their presence was a blessing.

The Rwandese people are a joyful people, and this quality is due not to their current circumstances but to an outpouring of faith in God. They are people who worship with a marked intensity. They are praying for God's healing hand to take away the trauma, to resurrect their lives, and to restore their country. Though most are stricken with poverty, I found myself envying their carefree stride and their contagiously social nature. Rwanda has had to skip several generations of technology, so though many homes are mud huts, most everyone has a cell phone. Talking is a favorite pastime. In Kigali, clusters of people stand on the street corners and in front of local merchants, engaged in laughter and tireless chatter. Friendly conversations fill the city's air with a lyrical quality all day long, even well into the night—the city is alive.

Through the days of my stay, I also learned that genocide is not easily understood, even for those who have lived through it. After reading Rwanda's history and personally interviewing victims, I found no clear explanation that satisfies. There are only so many words in the human language that can describe the obscenities of this massacre. Genocide survivors live with a duplicity that is not easy to understand. They have great hope, yet they cannot fully live with the assurance that genocide will not happen again. They are rebuilding their lives, but they cannot rebuild them fully without learning to trust again. The red, iron-fortified soil and the oversized fruit speak of their inherited blessings from heaven, but the very same ground was the host of thousands of hell's demons who trampled on all that was good.

Trauma still plagues survivors, and they remember details like genocide happened yesterday, though it's been fifteen years. I believe the depth of their trauma is more profound than we know, reconfiguring how they view humanity, God, and others. It's so deep that no matter how strong the government becomes, no matter how many new businesses go up, no matter how many Hutus reconcile with Tutsis, the answers they need in order to experience healing must transcend this world. The cure they need is a spiritual one.

Despite the odds of their history, I left with a deep certainty that the people of Rwanda would turn their country away from violence toward peace. Though they have endured three genocides, hope was yet the stronger force in their lives. And God is speaking to his people around the world to weep for them, to give generously, and to sacrificially join him in his work there. Americans are asking more and more about Rwanda, a country no bigger than the state of Maryland.

Families are being called to support the orphans. Missionaries are being called to love the people. I believe in the years to come, America will look to Rwanda as a very bright light of hope, a country that has been restored by the healing hands of God.

I had never been to a third world country before, so I was curious what greed might exist in conditions of poverty and what generosity could be found among people who have nothing to give. Universally it's true—no matter what our economic class, our race, or our gender might be, the truth is that goodness and greed are struggles we all have as humans. We are all connected by life's sufferings and life's joys, whether inflicted by our own sin or the sin of others.

The whole world needs faith to hope in God, and Rwanda has something to offer in that. My prayer is that the readers of this book come away with the hope of knowing that no evil can penetrate or devastate a life enough to snuff out the goodness of God. He is always greater still. I have witnessed this firsthand. "Hallelujah, our God reigns!"

Glossary

Rwanda: A country in East Africa that is approximately the size of Maryland, rich in agriculture. It borders Congo (west), Tanzania (east), Burundi (south), and Uganda (north) and is the most densely populated country in Africa. Kigali, the capital, is the largest city with approximately 9 million people. Rwanda was a united country before Belgian forces came in prior to World War I. Observing that the country was Tutsi-led, the Belgians declared them to be the superior race.

Genocide: The attempt to eradicate a people group based on their ethnicity, nationality, or religious belief system. The Rwandan genocide of 1994 lasted for approximately one hundred days; the government has recorded the death toll to be 1,074,017, which breaks down to approximately 10,000 murders every day. People were killed more quickly during these days than any other time in modern recorded history.

Rwanda has survived several genocides in the twentieth century, but 1994 was the most heinous. Killings began April 7, following the assassination of President Habyarimana.

Interahamwe: Hutu-led paramilitary organization. *Interahamwe* means "those who stand together" or "those who attack together." This militia group had the support of the Hutu-led government in Rwanda before and after the days of massacre.

Tutsi: Though the stereotype is not accurate, Belgian colonizers in the early 1900s identified this tribe as the more elegant Rwandans; they were taller, lighter-skinned, and thought to be the superior race, though they shared common culture and language with other Rwandans. This is based on "Hamitic" ideology, which is the belief that the Tutsi are descendants of Ham, son of Noah.

Hutu: Though the stereotype is not accurate, Belgian colonizers in the early 1900s identified Hutus as the "ordinary" Rwandan tribe; they were darker-skinned, had flat noses, and were thought to be less intelligent. In 1933, Belgians issued identity cards based upon body measurements: forehead length, nose width, etc. Though they declared Hutus to be of a different race, it was rather a political scheme intended to divide the country. (There is a small percentage of Twa, or bushmen, who also live in Rwanda.)

Rwandan Patriotic Front (RPF): Founded in 1987 by refugee Tutsis in Uganda, led by President Paul Kigame. Receiving no help from the United States during the Hundred Days, the RPF ended the violence of genocide. This military force is also the ruling political party of the country. Eric Irivuzumugabe has family members who have served as soldiers in the RPF. This heroic organization teaches Rwandese to see themselves only as "children of Rwanda," with no tribal distinctions.

Muhazi Lake: Also called "Mohasi," about twenty kilometers east of Kigali in the Rwamagana District. Some Tutsi tried to cross this lake using banana stems as rafts as their hunters pursued them. Though once a place of unimaginable violence, its tranquil waters now serve as a popular tourist spot in Rwanda.

Kinyarwanda: A tonal, Bantu language spoken in Rwanda. Along with English, it is one of the official languages of the country. Until recently, French was also considered to be one of the official languages.

Eric Irivuzumugabe is a Rwandan genocide survivor with a powerful story. His testimony is one of marked perseverance and hope, an account of what God can do when all has been lost. He is founder of Humura Ministries, a nonprofit organization formed to minister to the spiritual and physical needs of orphans and widows. Eric has cared for his two younger brothers since the genocide of 1994 and now cares for hundreds of orphans in the wake of his country's devastation, organizing conferences and discipleship groups. Eric lives in Kigali, where he works on staff as a chauffeur for Restoration Church. His hope is to work full time with Humura Ministries in the near future so he can devote more time to the restoration of the younger generations of Rwanda.

Tracey D. Lawrence (M.A., D.Phil.) is founder of Scribe Ink, Inc., specializing in collaboration, authoring, and book editing. Tracey has collaborated with Chuck Colson on various projects including *The Good Life* study guide, *Countercultural Christians*, and *Playing God? Facing Everyday Dilemmas of Biotechnology*. She has written for Gary Smalley on his project *Your Relationship with God*, as well as for ministries such as the Wilberforce Forum, BreakPoint, Focus on the Family, and others. She has authored or coauthored several book projects including *A Savvy Christian's Guide to Life*, and *Sister Freaks* and *Loved!* both with Rebecca St. James. She holds an M.A. in church history and theology and a doctorate in philosophy with an emphasis in social research. Tracey and her husband, Noel, have a son, Jack Brennan, and actively serve at Rocky Mountain Christian Church in Frederick, Colorado. She can be reached at tracey dlaw@aol.com.

About Humura Ministries

In 2005 Eric Irivuzumugabe founded Humura Ministries. With the help of a Board of Directors, Eric and a number of orphaned survivors of the 1994 Rwandan genocide have been ministering to fellow orphans in Rwanda.

Humura Ministries is a charitable trust organization designed to assist orphans in Rwanda. Their mission is to teach and proclaim the Good News of Jesus Christ, to assist the orphans of genocide and AIDS, and to promote the restoration of Rwanda.

For more information on Eric's ministry and how to invite Eric to speak at your event see:

www.irivuzumugabe.com

To send contributions to the ministry, make checks payable to:

Humura Ministries
P.O. Box 41
Little Chute, WI 54140